The Overnight Job Change Strategy

Donald Asher

Ten Speed Press

1

TEN SPEED PRESS
P.O. Box 7123
Berkeley, California 94707

Cover and text design, and typography by Fifth Street Design, Berkeley, California

Library of Congress Cataloging-in-Publication Data

Asher, Donald.
    The overnight job change strategy / Donald Asher.
        p.   cm.
    ISBN 0-89815-487-1
    1. Job hunting.   2. Career changes.   3. Job satisfaction.
I. Title.
HF5382.7.A84   1993
650.14 — dc20   93-29835
                                                                    CIP

FIRST PRINTING 1993

1 2 3 4 5 — 97 96 95 94 93

Printed in the United States of America

A Note from the Author

The only significant difference between people who do things and people who don't is exactly that. Pick up this book and do something to make your life better.

—Donald Asher

Donald Asher, President
Résumé Righters
San Francisco
(415) 543-2020

Mailing Address:

Donald Asher
The Overnight Job Change Strategy
c/o Ten Speed Press
P.O. Box 7123
Berkeley, California 94707

To Elizabeth Wingrove and Eric Schwaab, best friends who taught me the meaning and the value of their friendship.

Acknowledgements: Zig Ziglar of Zig Ziglar Corporation, Tom Hopkins of Tom Hopkins International, Norman King of American Marketing Complex, George Walther of George Walther, Inc., Richard Mueller of Welling & Woodard, and Sherrill Estes of Tri S Corporation helped me immensely with sales tips for jobseekers, as did Marc Kulkin, Richard Hirsch, Peter Chiang, Greg Saer, and several anonymous sales professionals. Without their honest input and freely offered secrets, this book would not have been as powerful or innovative. I am also indebted to Robert C. Chope, Ph.D., of Career Development Institute and Joe Meissner of Power Marketing for technical advice. Special thanks to Christine Lee, Marsha Keeffer, Anyika Nance, Patty O'Keefe, Andrea Miskow, Calvin Cheng, John Heed, Maureen Daly, and Danaelle Bell for contributions both material and emotional.

Some of the material in this book originally appeared in other forms in *From College to Career* and in the *Wall Street Journal*'s *National Business Employment Weekly* and *Managing Your Career* magazines. These sections are adapted by permission of Ten Speed Press and Dow Jones & Co., respectively.

Authors and works quoted in the chapter headings and in the text are used by permission of the publishers:

The Entrepreneur's Manual, by Richard M. White, Jr., by permission of the Chilton Book Company, Radnor, Pennsylvania.

Job-Search Supply Cabinet

○ 5 × 8-inch index cards to make lead cards (see p. 18)

○ 8½ × 11-inch stationery, for job-search letters: white, ivory, or light grey, 24 lb. minimum

○ 7¼ × 10½-inch stationery for shorter but still formal job-search letters

○ 5½ × 8½-inch or smaller stationery for handwritten notes

○ some formal thank-you cards, very conservative in style

○ résumés, customized for almost every mailing

○ 9 × 12-inch envelopes, preferably white, also known as "catalog envelopes"

○ regular envelopes to match your stationery

○ business cards; make your own "jobseeker" cards (see p. 16)

○ postage scale

○ answering machine or service, with formal outgoing message

○ fax capabilities, your own or easy access

○ word-processing capabilities, your own or easy access

○ a coherent wardrobe, to the last detail

Table of Contents

CHAPTER 1

A Job Search Is a Sales and Marketing Project

"Nothing ever happens until somebody sells something."
—Richard M. White, Jr., *The Entrepreneur's Manual*

You Are Both Entrepreneur and Sales Representative

As a candidate, you are like a small business with a product to sell and limited resources to expend in the most efficient manner possible. Like any entrepreneur launching a start-up company, you must take full responsibility for your own success or failure. You will have to do most of the jobs yourself, from discovering the best niche market for your product, to writing your own advertising copy, to identifying and accessing the key players and decision-makers in your targeted market, to making presentations on your product's features and benefits, to closing sales deals on profitable terms. At night you can keep the books and sweep up the shop.

As with any other small business, your seed money is limited. You cannot afford to make very many mistakes. Overhead ticks away like a time bomb. If you squander your resources, you will face one of the three consequences faced by any new company: you will be forced out of business by your creditors, be forced to sell your product for next to nothing just to create some cash flow, or, worst of all, be forced to sell your product to the wrong market and for the wrong end-use.

If you are a highly skilled worker, you are like an electronic instrument: complex and specialized, expensive, and hard to fix—the opposite of versatile. Your heavy duty instrument package might pick up a few bucks as a doorstop or a boat anchor, but your long-term strategic plans will be ruined or delayed by such a sale. When a worker takes a job below her potential, the same sort of thing happens; when a talented manager works as a security guard or a pot washer, we all lose, *even the other security guards and pot washers.*

This book is dedicated to the idea that you can seek and find the right job for you. Searching for a new job should not be mysterious. Like baking chocolate chip cookies or converting matter to energy, there is a proven formula for it. You are about to learn that formula. You can use this formula to plan, launch, and control a job search, whether you choose to search full-time or part-time, while you are still employed, or even at long-distance.

The Overnight Job Change Strategy or, Six Steps to Working Happiness
1. *Identify One or More Precise Job Targets*
2. *Identify Raw Leads*
3. *Develop Raw Leads into Specific Names to Contact*
4. *Turn a Name into an Appointment*
5. *Sell in the Interview*
6. *Close the Deal*

By breaking down the process into distinct components, you can see how easy it is to launch and operate a sophisticated, comprehensive, and ultimately successful job-search campaign. You can also solve job-search problems by identifying which component is the stumbling block, and by fixing only what is broken. The six steps above are the six central chapters of this book. The book is designed to be read first as a comprehensive overview of modern, aggressive, job-search techniques, and then later reread in chapters as needed, to serve as a problem-solver for specific stages of your search.

Sales & Marketing for the Neophyte

Every lesson from sales and marketing is directly transferable to job seeking. The techniques that lead to success in a sales campaign lead to success in a job-search campaign. The more you understand sales as a paradigm for the job search, the better and faster your search will go.

It is not enough to have a hot product. If you cannot sell it, it will rot or rust and you will go hungry.

Most job-seekers are lousy at selling their product. They use passive techniques that either involve excessive competition from other jobseekers, or fail to motivate the buyer at all. How much outrageously expensive perfume could you sell if you waited for someone to run an ad requesting, "Outrageously expensive perfume wanted by Friday night"? How many automobiles do you think you could sell if you waited for the consumer to advertise, "Sexy new convertible wanted cheap"? How many insurance policies could you sell if you waited for a small business owner to advertise, "$1,000,000 general liability policy needed by auto repair shop"?

Yet most job-seekers are willing to do just that. They wait until the employer (a) discovers a need, (b) defines that need in terms of a job, (c) seeks a candidate internally and informally, and finally, (d) runs an ad or places the position with a search firm. Anytime you wait for an announced opening before applying for a job, you are waiting

past the stages where you can make an easy sale. You are waiting for the competition, that lazy throng of job applicants that undoubtedly contains someone with one more year of experience and one more credential than you.

What you want to do is create demand for your product. You want to preempt the competition. You want to use active search techniques instead of tired old passive techniques.

CREATED DEMAND. That's the secret to sales. That's defining your product as the solution to someone's problem, sometimes before he even realizes he has a problem.

In a job search, that's accessing an employer as close as possible to point "A," when the employer discovers, or is about to discover, that he has a need. You create your own opportunity.

That's the hidden job market. Depending on which study you read, only 15 to 30 percent of all jobs are filled by someone who heard about the job because it was advertised, posted, or placed with a headhunter or employment agency. The other 70 to 85 percent are filled by individuals who learned about the opening from a friend or acquaintance, or just happened to be in the right place at the right time. The term "hidden job market" is really a misnomer. No one is purposefully hiding these jobs! Employers just don't need to announce most job openings *because they are filled before they have a chance to announce them.* Announcing a job opening costs money and delays the placement process, so employers won't announce openings if they don't have to. If you want to reach this preannounced job market, the overwhelming majority of all the jobs out there, you have to use sales techniques.

Do you have to be any good at sales? Absolutely not. You just have to *do* sales to succeed at it. You have to circulate in the right places, and sooner or later it will be the right time.

Take the example of the neophyte copier sales representative. She canvasses small businesses all day long trying to sell copiers. "How's your copier? Happy with it? Thinking about getting a new one?" If she is really new, she won't even realize that the average small business gets a dozen of these queries every single week of the year. Her success is not the result of her skill or sales talent—it is the result of her legwork and effort. Sooner or later someone's copier screws up for the umpteenth time, and "How's your copier?" is answered by "It's horrid. We're thinking about replacing it."

I knew a freelance writer who had no personal presence at all. She was shy, mousy, and demure. She didn't dress well and she never looked anybody in the eye. She wasn't even that good a writer. But she was never short of work. She had a card file of everyone she had ever met who would ever have the remotest chance of giving her a freelance writing assignment. Two weeks before she completed any job, she got out that file and started phoning, asking in her mousy tone if they had any projects they needed help with. She had no style but she had guts—and plenty of work.

This Book Is Not for Everybody

This book is designed to be of maximum benefit to the savvy candidate who has already made the mental decision to get a new position.

If you are looking for a primer or an encyclopedia on job searching, this book is not for you—it is too brief and many of the concepts and techniques are advanced. Some good primers and encyclopedias are listed in the bibliography.

In particular, if you are looking for a book to help you decide what you want to do next, careerwise, then this book is not for you. If you need psychoanalysis, aptitude testing, or several months' time off to recover from the stress of your last position, then you may not be ready for this book. This is a book about how to pursue a job, not how to decide which job to pursue. If you don't know what you want to do next, you will not succeed in your job search anyway. I recommend a careful reading of Bolles' *What Color Is Your Parachute?* Be sure to take the time to complete all the exercises as you come to them. Also try Bolles and Crystal's *Where Do I Go from Here with My Life?* or Gale's *Discover What You're Best At.* Of course, you can pursue individual career counseling or vocational/psychological testing. These services are available from most major universities (often whether you attended college there or not), and from professionals in major cities. The most important thing for you to do, however, is seek out and talk to people who have jobs and careers that interest you. Incidentally, you can refine your career goals with this book, as long as you have an idea of where you'd like to start. We'll go into this in greater detail in the next chapter.

If you are looking for a guide to help you conduct a passive job search, then this book is definitely not for you. It will make you feel guilty about being lazy and passive in your search, and it will constantly remind you of all the leads and opportunities you are missing. If you want to conduct such a search, which basically amounts to writing a résumé and sending out a few letters in response to ads in the paper or leads you may hear about casually, then by all means buy a good résumé book and start licking stamps. I suggest my book, *The Overnight Résumé,* which also has information on cover letters. For some people a passive search makes sense, especially those who really don't care if they find another position anytime soon.

If you are looking for a book to help you generate a mountain of good job leads, penetrate the screens around decision-makers, sell yourself in an interview, and close a series of job offers, then this book is for you. If you want to be able to troubleshoot your search, restart a stalled job search, and identify exactly what you may be doing wrong, then this book is for you. If you are a seasoned careerist who wants a quick guide to current techniques, then this book is for you. If you want to create your own "luck," then this book is for you.

What You Can Do Overnight

Although it is possible, it is overwhelmingly unlikely that you can get a new job overnight. What you can do overnight, however, is construct a sophisticated and comprehensive job-search plan: the Overnight Job Change Strategy. Candidates usually waste the first three weeks of their job search in false starts and missed opportunities. Even after they settle into the routine of their search, candidates usually apply 80 percent of their effort to techniques that turn up only 15 to 30 percent of all possible jobs.

This book is a black-box device; you go into it at one end with a desire for a new position and come out on the other end with multiple job offers. It gives you a template for an aggressive job-search campaign, fully equal to those that outplacement companies charge thousands of dollars to design. *The Overnight Job Change Strategy* incorporates the latest wisdom from headhunters and outplacement professionals, then goes beyond that to apply to the job search techniques used by sales and marketing pros. In addition to the proven techniques recommended to everybody, it offers more than a few advanced techniques for the brave and the few.

This book originated with my experiences as a professional résumé writer, career counselor, and coach in the job-search process. My service has traditionally focused on assisting fast-track professionals who engineer their own career paths, create their own success, and generally self-actualize their working life to suit themselves. I have worked with almost exactly 10,000 such individuals since I started in this business. The tips and techniques presented here have been tried and proven by these 10,000 highly motivated, highly intelligent, and creative people. They work—if you do.

CHAPTER 2

Identify One or More Precise Job Targets

"He flung himself from the room, flung himself upon his horse and rode madly off in all directions."
—Stephen Butler Leacock, *Gertrude the Governess*

Make a List of Target Statements

Before you fling yourself from the room and ride off in all directions, you need to define your job targets. Take out a pen and a pad of paper, because the "applied" part of this book begins right here.

Write down your immediate job objective as specifically as you can. List a **function,** such as sales or accounting, and an **industry**, such as aerospace or retail. Always define function first, industry second; function is what you are going to *do* all day, so it is much more important.

You cannot list a function alone, such as "sales," or an industry alone, such as "advertising." You need both function and industry, and you need to know an approximate title. A job is simply a conjunction of industry and function, but you need to know its name—its **title**—before you can apply for it or even talk about it. Select a typical title for the job you want, but do not worry too much about a specific title; one company's "comptroller" is another's "accounting manager."

Sometimes a candidate will even know exactly which **company** she is going to target first, but be careful not to confuse a company with a job. Define the job you want—industry and function—not just the company you want to work for. Candidates who target companies are at a distinct disadvantage; companies hire people to perform specific jobs, not people who just want any job. Besides, as you shall see as you progress through this book, no one targeted company should be allowed to dominate your job search.

You might also want to provide some indication of the specific **responsibilities** you are seeking, and some parameters for **salary** goals. You may have definite requirements in **scheduling**, such as a need for flextime or a preference for business travel.

You should anticipate the **size** of the organization you would be most comfortable in, but try not to exclude small or even tiny companies. Remember, job growth in this country is mainly driven by smaller companies.

Finally, you can list your **geographic parameters**. If you are only looking for work within a forty-minute commute or within the New York City metro area or "somewhere in the Pacific Northwest," let that be part of your immediate job objective.

Some of you will be able to be extremely specific right away, such as:

○ **Financial Aid Officer** for any Ivy League school, or a liberal arts college with both a strong academic reputation and sound fiscal standing.

Be as precise as you can. Instead of defining your desired function as "something in accounting," specify your goal as narrowly as possible, for example: "payroll accountant," "cost accountant," or "supervisory or department head position in a general ledger environment." Instead of defining your industry as "manufacturing," specify "plastic pipe manufacturing," "printed circuit board manufacturing," or "plastic molds and extrusion fabrication."

Do not mix up incompatible jobs, that is, do not lump together jobs that require different skills. Perhaps you have the skills to be either a recruiter or a benefits specialist. You will need to make a separate mission statement for each. *You might have several related and unrelated job targets, but each should be as specific and finite as you can make it.*

If you can identify at least one such precisely defined target, you can start your job search. If you cannot, you will not succeed in your search until you do.

Everything you do from here on out in your job search depends on a specific, articulated job target. Here are some more examples, as written by candidates like yourself performing this exercise:

○ Buyer in hard lines for a major department store.

○ Senior wastewater engineer (Engineer III) for a municipality in upper Michigan, night shift OK but not for more than the first few months.

○ Director of corporate communications for an insurance company. Salary target: $65K plus full perks absolute minimum. Prefer to have the media relations role and authority over an in-house print media design/production department.

○ Assistant manager of a restaurant with $2+ million annual sales, any location, any shift, but with potential for rapid advancement to unit general manager.

○ Senior-level sales position for an industrial supplies manufacturer/importer, possibly but not necessarily capitalizing on my knowledge of solvents and lubricants.

○ Office/administrative position at an advertising agency in New York.

○ CEO of a food manufacturing company with at least $50 million annual sales.

○ MIS director for a hospital. 24-hour on-call OK but need flextime.

Create one or more of these statements for yourself now. Do not read further until you have completed this step. Always incorporate the factors of function, industry, and title, and include other parameters—salary, responsibility, company size, schedule, geography—as appropriate. Each job target should be as distinct and coherent in and of itself as you can make it.

THE FAR SIDE By GARY LARSON

"OK, Mr. Hook. Seems you're trying to decide between a career in pirating or massage therapy. Well, maybe we can help you narrow it down."

IMPORTANT NOTICE: Do not assume that you will actually obtain one of the job targets you specify here. You need these mission statements to launch your search, but a rigid dedication to an immediate job objective is almost always a mistake. Creativity and flexibility are critical to success in the job-search process. However, you cannot begin the process until you can generate one or more of these fairly specific job targets.

Respect Career Paths

Try to avoid selecting an immediate job objective for which you are patently unqualified. I once worked with a candidate who was convinced that his astounding success in running a video rental shop qualified him to be a sales manager at a car dealership. Although he could easily have landed a position in car sales, he was sure that he belonged in management. "How hard can it be?" he asked, until I pointed out that he had no knowledge of spending a million dollars per year on advertising, no understanding of the legalities of finance and insurance, not a shred of experience in designing and directing sales training, and had never made more than $25,000 per year in his life.

This candidate could easily have *become* a car sales manager, earning a six-figure income at almost any major dealership, if he had taken a moment to consider the career path to that position. Although it is probably overwhelmingly obvious to you that he was going to have to sell a few cars first, this candidate was blind to the notion.

Most positions have career paths that feed into them and opportunities for advancement that feed out of them. If you intend to advance, you want to be constantly maneuvering into position for your next promotion and the promotion after that.

Plan Career Transitions

If you want to achieve a career transition, analyze it. In a management environment, most job changes involve fairly minor shifts in function and industry. For most candidates, *it is not possible to make a major shift in both function and industry in one career move.* If such a shift is your goal, plan on making a change in only one factor (either function or industry), and then making a second career move fairly rapidly after that, say within one year or maybe two years at the most. This is called "bouncing." Companies don't like it (at least the middle company in the equation) and no career books to date have been brave or foolish enough to recommend it, but savvy careerists know all about it.

For example, pick any major career shift, say from internal auditing in banking to direct outside sales for a pharmaceutical company. Here are two ways to achieve that:

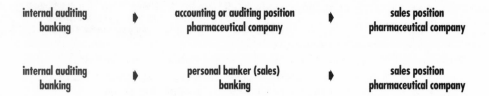

You can use the same technique to achieve a radical career shift and achieve a rapid return to a high level of responsibility. No one hires a department head from another industry, but someone might be very happy to hire an outsider to fill the number two slot. If the outsider is an aggressive careerist, however, she will be in that number two slot for as short a time as it takes her to convince another company to let her have a go at the number one slot. Here is an example:

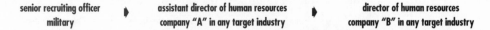

You should not stay in the middle position for more than two years, and you need to spend that time aggressively making contacts with players and companies in the next stage of your career transition. You may also need to pursue outside training to convince employers to take a risk on you in a function you have not performed before. Someone going from sales to accounting may very well need to take a few continuing education courses or even pursue a degree or certification with a university. Moonlighting is also a potential bridge between functions. A simplistic example: The internal auditor in the first diagram above could break a few records selling Avon or Tupperware to demonstrate sales skills. Of course it goes without saying that only strong performers will find these career transitions easy. Everybody wants talent, even if it is proven in another arena.

Using this formula for bouncing to achieve career transitions, you can segue from any job "A" to any job "Z" in a relatively systematic manner. The only exceptions are jobs for which you simply cannot enter the funnel. If you are over twenty-one and you have never taken ballet, there is nothing I can tell you that will help you become a ballet star. It's too late.

Do not assume you have to leave your current employer in order to launch a major career change. Often your own employer, who knows you best, will be more willing than a prospective employer to allow you to make a shift in function. If you work for a large and diversified company, you can achieve radical shifts in function and even industry without ever leaving the fold. When possible, this is to your advantage.

Incidentally, candidates of all types often fail to look carefully within their own organizations before leaving. Before you decide you have to leave, explore opportunities to meet your career goals in other departments or divisions, and in parent, subsidiary, and affiliated companies.

If you plan to make a career transition, you may have to accept a setback, sometimes a major setback, in your salary, geographic parameters, level of responsibility, or other immediate employment objectives. I have known candidates who took a 50 percent cut in pay in order to double their salaries subsequently, or took on a position in figurative Siberia to prove they could open a new office or territory. Ironically, *becoming a slave to your salary and perks can often arrest your career advancement.* Consider the whole picture, and if an immediate career transition truly serves your five-year goals, go for it.

How You Can Learn More About Career Paths

The very best way to learn about career paths and plot career transitions is to talk to people who have the job you want to have in five or ten years. Ask them how they got into it, what were the keys to their career advancement, what they would do differently if they had it to do over again, and what advice they have for someone with your background. People are almost always willing to talk about themselves. Be prepared for this conversation, however. The more you know about the industry and the position you want, the more someone like this can help you.

Start with people in your network, but expect to go beyond the people you know personally. You should be perfectly comfortable calling strangers to say, "I'm really interested in a career in _____, and I'd love to talk to you about how you got to where you are today. Do you have a couple of minutes right now, or is there a better time I should call?" (We'll cover telephone techniques in greater detail later.)

This is a classic example of what is meant by "informational interviewing," and job candidates never really outgrow the need for it. Even senior executives call each other for advice and counsel on prospective career moves. Don't be intimidated by the term "informational interviewing" and its cousin, "networking"; these are just more ways to say "talking to people."

All the material in the next two chapters on how to identify and develop leads also applies to identifying leads and obtaining appointments for informational interviews. If anything, it is easier to obtain a quick informational interview, if that is really all that you are after, than it is to proceed with the appropriate inquiries about a potential job. Do not abuse this, however, as people generally hate being tricked. Ever since Richard Bolles defined the informational interviewing process in his landmark book, *What Color is Your Parachute?*, naive candidates have been abusing the system.

Informational interviewing, when done properly, is not part of a job search; that is, it is not part of the process of applying for a job. It is, however, part of the preliminary investigations of a person who is considering in which direction to launch a job search.

Simply put: Informational interviewing is finding out about jobs—what a job is like—and job searching is finding out about job openings, potential openings, and leads to openings, that is, names of people who might know about openings. Do not be confused about which of these you are doing. You cannot excel at either by pretending to do the other.

If you come in asking for information to help you decide if you are interested in a particular career direction and uncover an opening, you are in a Catch-22. How strong a candidate can you be if only a few minutes ago you could not decide if you were even interested in this career direction? Think about it.

If, during the course of legitimate informational interviewing, you discover a promising job opening and you want to apply for it, do nothing. If you really are a good candidate, your contact will usually bring up the notion that you might want to apply. If he doesn't, and you are sure you want the position, say something like, "You know, this meeting really confirms everything I had hoped about _____. How would I go about making a formal application for the opening you mentioned earlier?" Then do what your contact suggests.

If you discover an opening but you are not stone-cold positive it is a good direction for you, you can easily say, "That opening you mentioned sounds interesting to me. If my other explorations confirm that this is the direction for me, you can bet that I'll be back in touch with you promptly."

You can use informational interviewing at any time during your job search. It is especially useful when you discover potential new directions that you had not really considered before. This happens even to seasoned executives in midcareer. Just be sure you know the difference between finding out what a job is like, and looking for a job. Act appropriately.

Although you should not use informational interviewing to pretend to look for a job, on the other hand you should never waste a contact. Get everybody's name, title, and phone number if possible. Ask for business cards. If you write down somebody's name, check the spelling. "Jon" sounds like "John," "Ann" sounds like "Anne," "Daly" sounds like "Daley," "Smythe" is often pronounced like "Smith." I even met a man once who spelled his first name "Donn."

What if You Don't Know What Direction to Pursue in the First Place?

If you are not sure of your career direction, you have two options available to you: arbitrarily decide on an immediate job objective, or launch a period of investigation and introspection to discover your true calling.

If you need to learn more about a specific industry or job function you think you might be interested in, you can use the techniques described in the above section to do that easily.

If you are unsure of what career possibilities might be appropriate for your personality, education, skills, and aptitudes, it will be worth it for you to take some vocational testing. Some of the most common tests are the Strong Interest Inventory, Myers-Briggs Type Indicator, California Psychological Inventory, and Minnesota Importance Questionnaire.

Vocational and aptitude testing are available from licensed psychologists and counselors who specialize in career issues, and often also from your local college or university's office of career planning and placement. Even if you did not attend the school, call the director of the career office and offer to pay a fee or make a donation to the university for the privilege of taking the tests and attending test orientation and interpretation sessions. Most will accommodate you. In major cities, I have seen advertisements in adult continuing education catalogs for these same tests. If such services are available near you, this is probably the cheapest way to take these tests.

You can also read your way into a new career direction. You might try *Discover What You Are Best At*, or try the exercises in *What Color Is Your Parachute?* or in *Guerilla Tactics in the New Job Market*. Three related books are *Work With Passion*, *Wishcraft*, and *Do What You Love, The Money Will Follow*. Finally, you can read about thousands of jobs in the U.S. Department of Labor's *Dictionary of Occupational Titles, vol. I, Definitions of Titles*, commonly known as the *DOT*, available in most libraries. (See Appendix and Bibliography for full publication data on these books.)

Another way to experiment with new career directions is to take workshops and adult education classes and attend lectures and public presentations in these areas.

This is comparatively cheap, fun, and easy. It is also a great way to get ideas for further inquiry and obtain reading lists of books related to your new interests. If you are not sure of your career direction, do *not* sign up for a degree program until you have dabbled in a few classes first.

Some people wake up one day in grade school and just *know* they want to be a chemical engineer. Other people wake up in a nursing home and still don't know what they want to do next. Most people fall somewhere in between these two extremes. In fact, in spite of their best intentions, most people have three or more completely distinct careers in their working lives. Be open to possibilities, but don't drift off into a sea of indecision.

Personally, I think too much is made of knowing *specifically* what you want in your next position. As a matter of fact, the strategies presented in this book will work better if you do not have a rock-solid set of specifications for your next position. Seeking a new position should be a process of discovery, and those who are flexible in their searches will be able to immediately capitalize on their findings as they go along. Being too rigid in your search can lead you to bypass a good opportunity, especially if it is something you had not anticipated.

One final note: Too much introspection can be a disaster if you are unemployed during your job search. You can go broke while you are trying to decide what you want to do with the rest of your life. My suggestion is that even if you are not totally sure, you should decide what your immediate career goal is, arbitrarily if necessary, and get going.

Query Letters to Use Early in a Job Search

When you want to find out more about a particular career option, you may want to use a query letter. Here are two examples, the first from a military officer planning a transition to the civilian sector, and the second from a seasoned candidate in business considering a major career shift. You can use these letters as guides to develop query letters to suit your own taste. Broadcast, networking, and cover letters are covered later in the book.

Sample query letter, military-to-business transition:

Dear Ms. Exactname:

After a successful career in the military, I am investigating potential careers in the civilian sector. I wonder if you could take just a moment to help me.

I am interested in learning about your industry, job titles, duties, and viable career paths within your field, and maybe hearing a few "war stories" about what it takes to get into and succeed in your arena.

My first preference would be a quick after-work meeting; the coffees or the drinks are on me. If you are simply too busy to arrange that, perhaps we could just chat on the phone, at your convenience.

I have enclosed my résumé so that you can get an idea of my background. (Don't worry—I'm not applying for a job. I just thought you might like a glance at it.)

Thank you for your consideration, and if I can return the favor someday, you can be sure that I will.

Sincerely,

Your Name Here

Sample query letter, major career transition in business:

Dear Mr. Exactname:

Once in a while, about once every ten years, I feel the need to strike out in a new direction. After considerable success in advertising and financial services (see attached résumé), I am eager for a new intellectual challenge.

I am interested in discussing career opportunities in your field. At this time I am not applying for a particular position. I am most interested in discussing your knowledge of trends in the industry, and possible contacts you may know who would be interested in someone with my background.

As you can see, I have a diverse background encompassing operations management, strategic marketing, and top-level representation to client presidents, CEOs, and government officials as needed. Due to my experience in Europe and Latin America, it is possible that a company seeking expansion into these markets would be interested in my skills in this area as well.

I'll give you a call within 48 hours of your receipt of this letter. I look forward to speaking with you soon, and I certainly appreciate any information you can give me.

Sincerely,

Your Name Here

Pick a Primary Job Objective

Before continuing on to the next chapter, review your job objective statements. Rank them in rough order, picking those you want to pursue immediately and placing them at the top, and those you may want to approach later in your search down near the bottom.

Finally, pick one precise job target as your **primary job objective**. In the following chapters we will focus on only one objective at a time. The intensive search techniques espoused in this book will not work without such focus, *even if that focus is arbitrarily applied.* You need to choose one target as your primary example and use it consistently as you read on.

For the duration of the book, and for that matter the duration of your job search, it is assumed that you have a clearly defined mission statement, a precisely articulated immediate job target to guide all your efforts and activities.

You May Wish to Make a "Jobseeker" Business Card

If you are currently employed and plan to continue your career in the same industry, you can just use your current business card for the duration of your search. If you are not employed, however, or if you plan a major career transition, it can be beneficial to have business cards that reflect your status.

Once you have defined your primary job objective, you can design and order "job seeker" business cards listing your name, address, and phone number and highlighting a functional title. Although I have seen business cards that literally list the title of "Job seeker," more descriptive titles reflecting your job objective or the expertise that you have to offer are much more productive. Use such descriptive titles as "Cost Accounting," "Real Estate Sales Professional," "Civil Engineer," "Market Research," or even such mini-advertisements as "Catering Assistant — On Call for You 24 Hours a Day."

The reason you want to have and use such cards in your job search is that cards have a much longer survival rate than letters and résumés. Long after letters and résumés have been relegated to the filing cabinet or waste bin, business cards will be sitting in plain sight on a cluttered desk, or safely within reach in a Rolodex file.

CHAPTER 3

Identify Raw Leads

*"Knowledge is of two kinds. We know a subject ourselves,
or we know where we can find information upon it."*
—Samuel Johnson, in Boswell's *Life of Samuel Johnson*

Types of Job Leads

T he best job lead is a **hiring authority,** someone who is personally able to hire you. Second-best is a **direct referral source,** someone who is personally able to refer you to a hiring authority. All your search efforts should be directed at identifying and accessing these two types of people. (Incidentally, every person in the world is an **indirect referral source.** Everyone you meet, or have ever met, should be considered an asset to your job search. We'll come back to this in a later section, "Networking = Talking to People.")

A **developed lead** is the exact name of someone you want to contact, along with her title, business address, and daytime telephone number. Anything else is a **raw lead**. A raw job lead may be a person's name—perhaps even that of a hiring authority or a direct referral source—but more commonly it is just a company's name. Of course, to be of any use to you, it must be a company that harbors the type of job you targeted in the last chapter.

Almost all raw leads, from rumors about companies to sparse listings in business directories, can be developed into lists of specific people, that is, names, titles, addresses, and daytime telephone numbers for hiring authorities and direct referral sources.

We will learn how to develop raw leads into complete listings in the next chapter. In this chapter our goal is to be sure that you know how to systematically generate an unending series of raw leads. Unless you can originate a large volume of job leads, your search can stall before you start to get job offers.

Lead Cards

Record your leads at the earliest opportunity on 5 × 8-inch index cards. Your job-search supply cabinet should always have two or three hundred extra 5 × 8-inch cards in it.

Be sure to list the name, title, and daytime phone number of your targeted contact, if you have these data (if you don't, the next chapter will teach you how to generate them). Note the exact source of the lead (the precise person, magazine article, or overheard conversation that gave you that lead) and the date each card was created. Finally, note any helpful inside information, such as, "Jane said he's always at his desk by 6:00 A.M.," or "Business Week article said they are expanding market share in Florida."

Work like a journalist! Get the exact spelling of names and titles. Record exactly which issue of *Business Week* the article was in. Verify the obvious, "Is that Glen with one 'n' or two?" Be sure to find out whether Leslie, Chris, or Gene is a Mr. or a Ms. Obtain full addresses at the earliest possible opportunity. Your careful attention to detail here will save you much time and trouble later.

These 5 × 8-inch cards can be sorted easily and are large enough to record a reasonable amount of data. Once you start contacting your leads, you will need room to note the exact date, time, nature, and result of each contact. A sample lead card appears on this page.

WALTON, Samuel (goes by "Sam")
Wal-Mart, Admin. HQ
11901 S. Hwy. 71
Bentonville, Arkansas 72715
(501) 555-1234

Résumé and letter sent 1/10/93. Follow-up phone call 1/12/93. Sam Walton is deceased! Talked to exec. sec. "Chris Spencer" She referred me to D.R. Wallace (goes by "D.R."). (501) 555-1279.

1/12/93.   8 A.M. D.R. Wallace "in a meeting." Left message.
1/13/93.   8 A.M. D.R. Wallace "unavailable." Left message.
1/14/93.   8:30 A.M. D.R. out of town until Monday. Asked D.R.'s secretary, Cathy Spencer (sister to Chris), if she had received résumé in her office. She said no. I said I'd send another and it would be on her desk before Monday.
1/19/93.   9:05 A.M. Reached D.R. Liked résumé, but wasn't sure when he would be in Dallas. I said I'd drive up to Bentonville. Meeting scheduled for Sat., 1/24/93!

Four Main Sources for Job Leads

BIZARRO By DAN PIRARO

I HATE TO WORRY YOU, DARLING, BUT I AM BEGINNING TO FEEL A LITTLE PRESSURE TO RESIGN.

There are four basic sources for raw job leads:

○ Friends and acquaintances, also known as networking leads.

○ Research, or the systematic identification of companies that harbor the types of jobs you have targeted.

○ Newspapers, bulletin boards, newsletters, your state's employment development department, and other places where job openings are advertised or posted.

○ Headhunters and employment agencies, which provide more or less exclusive referrals to companies, usually in relation to specific openings.

To keep it simple, let's label these four lead sources like this:

○ **Networking**

○ **Research**

○ **Newspapers and other sources for announced openings**

○ **Headhunters and agencies**

In a strict sense, job openings placed with headhunters and agencies, even exclusively, should be counted as announced openings. These jobs have already been defined in terms of an ideal candidate, and informal and internal efforts to fill these positions have already failed.

Most nonsystematic jobseekers put their energy and effort into only one or two of these lead sources. The most common error is to focus job-search efforts on announced openings, the latter two categories. This is a terrible way to look for work! Candidates miss 70 to 85 percent of all job opportunities by focusing on announced openings.

This is not to say that you should not pursue jobs in the newspaper or that you should fail to take that call from a headhunter. Absolutely you should pursue these avenues, *but with no more than 30 percent of your total job-search effort.* No one should launch an all-out job search without purposefully and systematically pursuing leads in all four categories. That is precisely what this book is all about: a systematic and thorough job search.

Networking = Talking to People

Networking is a fancy way to say "talking to people." When people say you should network, they mean you should talk to people. That's all they mean, nothing more and nothing less. First, you need to make a list of all the people to whom you can talk. These people do *not* need to be friends, or even acquaintances, just any and all people with whom you have enough of a common thread to initiate a conversation. If you can pick up the phone and call them, *for any reason,* they are potential networking contacts. Using this loose definition, most people have hundreds, perhaps even thousands, of contacts.

Most candidates do not understand networking. Your contacts don't have to be people who *obviously* can help you. Don't say to yourself, "How could Aunt Mabel know anything about biochemical engineering?" Give Aunt Mabel a chance to tell you that she just invested in an IPO for Nuvomedico, and her stockbroker just happens to know the company founder personally. Happy accidents are the rule, rather than the exception, when you network aggressively.

Everyone in the employment business can cite dozens of stories about how somebody's daughter's teacher's friend knew the wife of the bridge partner of somebody, and the result was a job placement. According to social scientists and epidemiologists, everyone in the world is only six acquaintances away from anyone else. Obviously, referrals can be a powerful component of a systematic job search. Aggressive job searching requires talking to a lot of people about your job search. (Of course, anybody who is still employed will wish to exercise some discretion.) You never know how these connections can come together, and you should not discount people who do not outwardly appear to be able to help you.

As an example, I know a San Francisco-based couturier who wanted to break into wardrobe design for the film business in Los Angeles. First she asked all her society patrons if they knew anybody in the film business. She got a few good leads, but nothing truly promising. She didn't stop there; she talked to cab drivers, to doormen, to the man who ran the corner store. In each case, she explained her interest in wardrobe design and asked, "Do you know anybody in the film business?"

One day in the gym with her personal trainer, an energetic woman and a fanatical trainer but a recent émigré who barely spoke English, she asked that question. "Oh, yes. I know a man in the film business. I met him on an aeroplane. He absolutely loves San Francisco. Every time he is in town we work out together."

"Oh," my friend said, "and what does he do?"

"He is, how do you call it? chief finance guy, for Major Films. I have his number if you want." Needless to say, she wanted it. The couturier flew to Los Angeles and was introduced to the film business from the executive suite down.

In a recent newspaper article, I read about a candidate who mentioned his job search to his garbage collector, who told him that the man who lived in the house on the corner was an executive at a company on the candidate's target list. The next Sunday, the candidate struck up a conversation with the executive on his front lawn. The following week the candidate was interviewed formally, and ended up being hired. The candidate's predawn comment to his garbage man led to a management-level placement. That's networking.

Here are some of the people you should let help you with your job search:

Ten Sources for Networking Contacts

1. **Family members,** close and not so close, near and distant.
2. **Friends,** current and former, close and not so close, near and distant, *and the members of their families.*
3. **Acquaintances,** current and former, even if when you call it takes a moment for them to remember who you are.
4. **Employers, coworkers,** supervisors, subordinates, colleagues, both current and former.
5. **Clients** and **customers** of current and former employers.
6. **Vendors,** suppliers, business venture partners, and friendly competitors—basically anyone you have ever talked to on the phone in a business setting.
7. **Classmates, professors,** and **teachers** from every school you have ever attended.
8. **Club members**—every member of every business, fraternal, or social organization you have ever belonged to.
9. **Church members**—every member of every church, temple, mosque, or ashram you have ever belonged to.
10. **Neighbors,** current and former.

And all **their** *friends and acquaintances!*

Before continuing in the book, take out a pad of paper or a stack of lead cards and make lists of as many people as you can in each of these ten categories. Just catalog these "human resources" for now; don't contact them until you have completed the next two chapters, "Develop Raw Leads into Specific Names to Contact" and "Turn a Name into an Appointment." Try to get member rosters for churches and clubs, and be sure to call your college's alumni office or office of career planning. You can usually get at least a directory of your fellow graduates, and often you can get leads and referrals to alumni in your targeted field. Depending on the loyalty of alumni, these can be a gold mine. Even if you graduated over twenty years ago, do not fail to call your alma mater's office of career planning and placement.

Remember, study after study proves that more jobs are filled by someone who found out about the position from someone they knew than from any other single source. Take this seriously, and above all, be systematic.

PERFORMANCE STANDARD: Don't settle for fewer than one hundred networking leads in all these categories combined.

Research Companies to Make Target Lists of Potential Employers

After you compile your lists of networking contacts, you should make lists of companies you will target in your search. You may have a few of these companies already in mind from your work in the last chapter. Only target those companies that harbor the type of jobs you want. Be systematic and be exhaustive.

Think beyond the obvious! For example, if you were interested in a traffic position in advertising, identifying and listing full-service ad agencies would only be a place to start. You would also want to identify and list in-house ad agencies, full-service marketing agencies, in-house corporate marketing departments, and even major corporate communications departments, all of which also hire traffic managers.

By now you can see how important it is that you have at least one specific job target in mind when you launch your search. If you don't know your goal, you simply cannot pursue it. Although you should be ready to refine your job objective and let the goals of your search evolve as you learn more about specific companies, positions, and job market conditions, you have to have a definite starting place. If you don't know the names of any specific companies, put down the type of company. You can turn any idea into a list of companies using plain old-fashioned research.

Although your initial research requires no more than a phone book, many of the resources you will need are available only at a public library. Plan on visiting the library at least once a week during your job search. There is simply too much good reference material there, and your friendly reference librarian is waiting to assist you. Reference librarians like to search for obscure data. They actually want to help you find out how many ichthyological research centers are in Oregon, Washington, and Idaho, or which companies in New Jersey are licensed to transport or dispose of radioactive materials. Remember going to the library as a kid? Going to the library to do career research can be just as magical.

Phone Numbers for the Reference Desk at Major Libraries	
New York Public Library	(212) 930-0800
Free Library of Philadelphia	(215) 686-5300
Chicago Public Library	(312) 747-4090
San Francisco Public Library	(415) 557-4400
Boston Public Library	(617) 536-5400
Miami-Dade Public Library	(305) 375-2665
Dallas Public Library	(214) 670-1400
Library of Congress	(202) 707-5000

Incidentally, you may be able to use the nearest university's career library whether you attended that school or not. Almost all offices of career planning and placement (CP&P) will honor a request for reciprocity. (You may need to obtain a letter from your alma mater's CP&P office requesting reciprocity and acknowledging you as a graduate.) You will need to be a self-starter, able to conduct your own research unassisted, for these offices are usually grossly understaffed and already overworked in serving their primary constituency.

Ten Sources for Company Names

1. **Yellow pages.** The resource of first resort.

2. **General job guides** citing employers by industry, size, and other categories. Usually too general and focused on very large employers, but a place to start (see below).

3. **Geographic job guides** citing employers in a specific city or metro area. An excellent place to start if you are new in town or looking for work in a distant city.

4. **Industry directories, association member rosters,** or **mailing lists.** These can be gold mines of data, providing everything from size and sales rankings to lists of key company officers.

5. **Trade press**. The trade press are publications that cover a specific industry. Every industry, from bartending to mechanical engineering, has its own publications. You *must* monitor the trade press in your targeted area.

6. **Popular press.** Although not as focused as the trade press, articles in the popular press, from *Forbes* to *Time* to the business section of your local paper, can provide large numbers of job leads.

7. **Chamber of commerce data**. Most chambers collect enormous amounts of data on local businesses, and often compile rosters or directories by specific categories.

8. **Database companies and information brokers**, local or national.

9. **Telephone research**. Determine who would be able to give you names of companies in a particular category, then just call them and ask.

10. **Field research**. If all the car dealers or high tech manufacturing companies are in a certain part of town, just drive around and write down their names.

Be sure to research every company's competitors, suppliers, and customers, too!

If you need telephone directories for distant cities, they can be found at your local library or at the nearest major airport. If you know anyone in the city you have targeted, he may be able to mail you a copy of that city's yellow pages. You can buy a telephone directory for any city in the United States by calling Pacific Bell Telephone at 800-848-8000 or 209-383-6655.

General job guides are books like *Everybody's Business: A Field Guide to the 400 Leading Companies in America, The 100 Best Companies to Work for in America, America's Fastest Growing Employers,* and *The Best Companies for Women.* Some general business books are also quite useful for jobseekers, such as *Standard & Poor's Register of Corporations, Directors, & Executives.* Geographic job guides list employers in specific major metro markets, such as Seattle or New York. Some job guides cover a specific industry, instead of a specific locale, such as *Career Opportunities in Television, Cable and Video.* A trip to the special order desk of any good bookstore or a call to the nearest reference librarian can tell you if there are job guides for your industry. Also see the appendix, "Resources You Can Use to Research Potential Employers," for more information on these types of resources.

Industry directories are published by trade associations, some government and regulatory agencies, and some publishing houses. Call or visit the reference desk of your local library and ask for the Guide to American Directories or Directories in Print. Here are just a few examples of the type of directory you should be seeking: International Directory of Marketing Research Houses, American Apparel Manufacturers Association Directory, American Electronics Association Directory, Working Press of the Nation, World Directory of Pharmaceutical Manufacturers, The Biotechnology Directory, and similar ad infinitum. Again, see the appendix, "Resources You Can Use to Research Potential Employers," for more information on these types of resources.

For the duration of your job search be sure to read the trade press, business press, and popular press for ideas and leads on companies. There is a special interest magazine or newsletter for everything and everyone in America, from carnivals to college professors. Read trade and business press for information on companies, market trends, hot growth areas, and companies to avoid. The popular press is less useful at providing business leads, but can be more useful at providing ideas in other areas, such as politics, sports, and the arts. If you don't know the names of the trade publications serving your field, look in *The Gale Directory of Publications* or *Business Periodicals Index*. Finally, as far as print resources go, you need to know about the mothers of all job research guides, the *Job Hunter's Sourcebook: Where to Find Employment Leads and Other Job Search Resources*, which has a good section on trade press, and the *Encyclopedia of Business Information Sources*, which covers periodicals, directories, and associations by industry.

Although you probably should not delegate the honest hard work of generating leads, there are database companies and information brokers that will do that work for you. Fees and services vary, but you can, for example, ask for a list of all the petrochemical companies in New Jersey that have more than 1000 employees. Here are three companies providing job-search database services:

○ Seagate Associates, 201-262-5200 or 800-992-5520

○ Dun & Bradstreet Information Services ($300 minimum order), 201-605-6000 or 800-624-5669

○ Finders/The Advantage, 301-788-0500 or 800-628-9685

You can also look in the yellow pages under "information" in any major metro area. Some libraries have on-line systems that are particularly useful for jobseekers, providing data by industry and by company, complete with company profiles, names of key officers, and citations of recent newspaper articles for further research. Call your local library or check in *The Fiscal Directory of Fee-Based Information Services in Libraries* (published by FYI, a department of the County of Los Angeles Public Library, 310-868-4003 or 800-582-1093).

Incidentally, I have known jobseekers who hired college students to identify and investigate leads and generate other job-search data for them. If you have very little time and can afford it, having a college student "on retainer" for research, errands, and other legwork can be beneficial for you both. Some candidates who have grown used to having an attentive staff feel naked and abandoned without one. Hiring temporary clerical and gofer help is a cheaper and more reasonable solution than you might at first think.

✺

WARNING: Remember that all these print and database resources are only places to begin your research. You will still need to *develop* every lead, as discussed in the next chapter. These sources, like all reference sources, are obsolete before they are published. Although some of these books and database services try to be helpful by providing the exact name and address for various company officers and hiring managers, you cannot use one single bit of information without verifying it first by telephone. If you write to the president who was just fired, or to the address where the headquarters used to be, or concerning the division that was spun off, or to a company that is now going bankrupt, you reveal yourself to be a very poor candidate indeed.

✺

Anytime you cannot find what you want using the above methods, you probably need to use telephone and field research techniques. As any journalist will tell you, the best way to find any piece of information in the world is to decide or discover who would know, then call her and ask her. That's telephone research, and it is easy if you can articulate exactly what it is you want to find out, and you know how to use your telephone. Generally speaking, jobseekers tend to underutilize their telephones and rely overmuch on written communiques.

Field research is the same thing, but without a telephone. Simply go visit the person or the place that can provide the information you are seeking. Job fairs are an example of field research, but I think trade shows are even better. If there is a trade show in your field within a day's drive and you can buy or wangle an entrance pass, go. You can walk up to anybody's booth, introduce yourself, and pump the reps for all kinds of information. Collect cards, and get their recommendations on whom to contact at their firms. In my opinion, a savvy jobseeker at a trade show is like a fox in the henhouse while the dog and farmer are gone hunting. One jobseeker I know bought a "one day" ticket to attend the opening mixer at an industry convention. He couldn't afford to attend the whole convention but he got dozens of good leads this way, and he got a copy of the attendees' roster.

Here's another example of telephone and field research: A client of mine recently mentioned an interest in wholesale sales of golf equipment. He was an avid golfer with a distinguished career in financial sales, but not one idea how to approach this new industry. "Why don't you just call two or three pro shops and ask them how to get into equipment sales?" I suggested. He called me the next day to let me know that in three phone calls and one visit to a pro shop he had been able to compile a list of suppliers, the names of their sales managers, and solid intelligence on which companies were good or bad to work for. Three days in the library would not have yielded this much useful information.

❋

Finally, remember that every company has competitors, suppliers, and customers. If you have industry-specific knowledge that would qualify you for a position with Company A, you probably have industry knowledge that would be of interest to most of Company A's competitors, suppliers, and customers. Unless your entire industry is in a precipitous decline, the number one source of good targets is your most recent employer's major competitors.

Think systematically! A major problem for many jobseekers is that they flit from one lead to the next, one target to the next, without generating any cumulative knowledge from their search efforts. I know of one college graduate who wanted to find a job as a property manager. He was too young and had almost no experience that could even remotely be construed as related to this career goal, but he was persistent and systematic. He identified every large and small property owner in his geographic target area, and applied to them in sequence. He timed his effort so that he always had at least ten active applications going. Whenever a potential employer rejected his candidacy, for whatever reason, he called them and asked three questions: what did they look for in a property manager, what could he do to improve his candidacy, and what could he do to improve his chances of getting a job like this in the near future. In this way he sharpened his candidacy, refined his understanding of the targeted employers, learned the lingo, improved his résumé, and began to get offers. He eventually got a fantastic job, *one that he never could have landed when he first started his search.*

Another candidate, a sales professional, answered an ad in the paper for a position repping little plastic wire hangers used in computers and other electronic equipment. After three interviews she learned about as much as you'll ever want to know about little plastic wire hangers. In the end, however, the company hired one of the other candidates. Instead of going on to apply for the next industrial sales job she heard about, say selling lubricants or insulators, this candidate researched and identified every other manufacturer of the little doohickeys. She used her new insider's knowledge to land a job with one of them. The last time I saw her, she was happy to report that she was gaining market share on the company that had failed to hire her.

❋

PERFORMANCE STANDARD: The number of company leads you can generate will vary tremendously depending on what industry and job you are targeting, where you want to live, and other restrictions you may place on your search. You should be able to generate *as a minimum* several dozens of leads to start with! Some jobseekers will be able to generate many *thousands* of leads using basic research techniques. Your goal, within reason, is to make a list of *100 percent* of the employers with the potential to hire you. Build a big lead list, and plan on contacting several companies simultaneously, not just one at a time.

Start with companies you know about already, then research your way through every applicable source for company names. Remember, don't overload your list with large companies. Over 60 percent of all jobs in America today are in companies with fewer than 250 employees.

Don't worry if your lists start to overlap, for example, if some of your networking contacts work at companies you wish to target. That just makes your job easier in the coming phases of your search.

Newspapers & Other Sources for Announced Openings

Many employment professionals have an unwarranted bias against advertised jobs; they fear that they must be low paying and unattractive, or the company would not have had to resort to advertising. In reality, however, many companies have no choice but to advertise. Small, off-the-beaten-track companies may not have a steady flow of applicants from which to choose, and any company needing an unusual combination of skills may be forced to announce an opening eventually. Finally, some companies and government agencies are required by policy to advertise all their openings.

The truth of the matter remains that once a job is advertised, it is highly likely that dozens, and sometimes hundreds or even thousands of applicants will be competing for the same opening. You need three things to win an advertised job:

○ A good match between your background and the employer's requirements.

○ An outstanding résumé and cover letter.

○ Precision performance at every stage of the application process.

Because of the heavy competition, newspapers can be a particularly poor source of job leads, however, they *are* worth pursuing.

Check the paper on Sunday for professional jobs, every day for lower-level jobs. You can usually buy the Sunday paper, want ads and all, on the Friday or Saturday before. If you are inexperienced or expect a lot of competition, timeliness is critical. Get your application in the mail on Saturday so it will be the first to arrive, or, better yet, hand deliver it yourself as soon as the company opens on Monday morning. Don't just drop it off and run; ask for an interview, that day if possible, and let them know you'd be happy to wait until one is available.

Although the above approach is one of the very best for getting entry-level positions, a manager using such an approach would seem desperate. We'll cover more sedate responses to announced openings in later chapters.

Check the Tuesday *Wall Street Journal* (the edition in which new ads traditionally debut) or subscribe to the *WSJ*'s *National Business Employment Weekly*, which combines a week's worth of ads from all four regional editions of the *WSJ* with topical articles on management-level job-search tactics; call 800-JOB-HUNT or 413-592-7761 to subscribe. You might also try *The National Ad Search*, a weekly compendium of want ads from seventy-five newspapers; call 800-992-2832 or 414-351-1398 to subscribe. If you are interested in employment in a distant city, be sure to subscribe to at least the Sunday edition of that city's dominant newspaper. Call today and subscribe. (If you want to save money, most libraries have a reading room with business periodicals and newspapers from major cities.)

Newspaper help-wanted ads are only one source for announced openings. Job openings are also announced on computer bulletin boards, profiled in obscure industry newsletters, listed with your state's employment development department, on record at the nearest federal Office of Personnel Management, recorded on company job hot lines, and posted on job bulletin boards in places as diverse as the local YMCA and your alma mater's office of career planning. Strategically, all these job leads should be treated as want ads.

In some cases it can even pay to monitor small local community papers. Some companies intentionally advertise lower-level jobs in such papers to reduce the applicant pool and find employees who will not have to commute very far. Other organizations, often nonprofit, political, and arts organizations, advertise in small special interest publications to recruit candidates with an existing interest in their cause. Finally, many companies that announce openings choose to do so exclusively in highly targeted professional publications. To be sure you are not missing a good job newsletter for your chosen field, check in one of the following resources: Where the Jobs Are: A Comprehensive Directory of 1200 Journals Listing Career Opportunities or Job Hunter's Sourcebook: Where to Find Employment Leads and Other Job Search Resources.

Remember, your goal in reading the want ads is not just to find an announcement for your ideal job, but to discover companies that might harbor the position(s) you have targeted. In reading want ads, read between the lines. If the company is recruiting a director of procurement, you can bet that soon there will be a variety of staff adjustments throughout the purchasing department. If a company is advertising for a French and German translator, they may be interested in penetrating EC markets. If a company is hiring several new employees at once, it is either growing rapidly or undergoing an internal reorganization. An intelligent person can discover and apply for all types of jobs by extrapolating from newspaper ads, especially those for management and executive personnel. Note that with this strategy, want ads that are months old are still pertinent to you.

Of course you should apply for advertised positions for which you are qualified, but the most fruitful approach is to treat want ads (and announced openings of all types) as just one more source of information on companies.

We'll discuss how to crack blind box ads in the next chapter.

CAUTION: Although every candidate should monitor help wanted advertising and other sources for announced openings, *no candidate should devote more than 25 percent of his effort to this source!* We'll consider the optimum mix of job-search effort in greater detail in chapter 5, "Turn a Name into an Appointment," and again in chapter 8, "Track and Troubleshoot Your Job Search."

PERFORMANCE STANDARD: Every candidate should monitor at least one major newspaper's want ads, and also research and subscribe to any job newsletters particular to her field. Some entrepreneurs provide job ad clipping services, mostly on a local basis. If you find a good one, call me and I'll list them in the next edition of this book: Donald Asher, 415-543-2020.

Headhunters & Agencies

You should always take a headhunter's call, and by all means try to give her a referral if you are not interested in the opportunity yourself. However, if you need to change jobs *now*, headhunters are an unlikely source for your next position. The maxim is, "Headhunters find people for jobs, not jobs for people." No matter how impressed a headhunter may be with you, she can do nothing for you if you do not fit one of the jobs she has on active search.

As a related point, you won't get much help from headhunters if you are attempting a career transition. Their job is to find somebody who is already an accomplished performer in the industry and function specified by the job listing.

Additionally, headhunters are paid vast sums of money to identify and access candidates that would otherwise be inaccessible to the employer. If you are unemployed, or about to be reorganized out of your company, you are simply not seen as such an elite property. We will discuss this further later in the book, but if you are unemployed, spending more than 5 or 10 percent of your job-search effort on headhunters is perhaps unwise.

There are two kinds of headhunting firms, although the division is not as strict as some firms might want you to think. **Contingency** headhunters obtain job orders from companies and then seek candidates to fill those specific openings. Contingency firms are paid only if the search results in a placement of a candidate whom they have advanced for the position. Companies may offer job orders to a contingency headhunter on an exclusive or a competitive basis. As you might imagine, if a job order is listed with several contingency headhunters, time is absolutely of the essence. If you take several days to polish up your résumé and fax it in to the headhunter, the opening might be long gone, filled by the headhunter who called you or a competing firm. Contingency firms may or may not do a background check on the candidate. They tend to concentrate on middle-management positions, but may take search orders for positions paying anywhere from $35,000 to well into six figures.

Retainer firms are retained on an exclusive basis to identify, investigate, and evaluate candidates for higher-level positions. Retainer firms are paid for their consulting services, which means they are paid whether a placement project is ultimately successful or not. Such firms try to concentrate on positions that pay close to or more than six figures, but may conduct searches for positions paying even less than $60,000.

In practice, retainer firms will occasionally accept a contingency assignment, and contingency firms will occasionally negotiate a retainer assignment.

In most states there is no legal difference between an employment **agency** and a headhunting firm. Working like contingency headhunters, agencies tend to place office staff and lower-level professionals, positions with annual salaries usually well under $60,000. Agencies are often much more willing to do job development for you; in other words, if they like you they might call around and try to obtain interviews for you even if they do not have an active search for someone with your skills. Headhunters are much less likely to do this, but it is possible if you are a hot property.

Agencies tend to be listed under "Employment Agencies" or "Personnel Consultants" in the yellow pages, and headhunters tend to be listed under "Executive Search Consultants" or unlisted in order to keep from being pestered by unsolicited contacts from unsavvy jobseekers.

Contingency headhunters and agencies in theory compete for job orders in the salary range of $35,000 to $60,000. In practice, however, most firms specialize in certain fields, such as legal secretaries or sales professionals, and most orders placed with search firms are not also floating around in agencies, and vice versa.

✳

For a list of agencies, look in the yellow pages or call your local chamber of commerce. First, try to pick out any agencies that have names that would indicate that they would handle someone in your field. Unfortunately, for every firm that clearly identifies its specialty with a name like Bilingual Secretaries Unlimited, there will be fifty firms with names like Johanson, Spight & Gaul. You have to call and survey them with questions like this, "Could you tell me which agencies in town are specialists in placing medical office personnel?" In many cases, your next question will have to be something like, "If you are the best, which agencies would you say are the second and third best in this particular niche?"

A full listing of contingency and retainer headhunters can be found in Kennedy's *Directory of Executive Recruiters.* Check your library or order your own from Kennedy Publications, 603-585-2200 or 603-585-6544. The Recruiting & Search Report (a publishing company) provides headhunter directories in over ninety industry and functional categories, and also provides custom database printouts for any major metro area in the U.S.; call 904-235-3733 or 800-634-4548. Don't forget that headhunters are not necessarily geographically dependent; a headhunter in Chicago may place a candidate from Miami in a position in Minneapolis. To learn more about headhunters in general, read *The Headhunter Strategy* or *Rites of Passage at $100,000+,* both excellent books. (More are listed in this book's bibliography.)

CAUTION: You must take great care in approaching headhunters. Be sure to read the headhunter portion of the next chapter before you contact any recruiting firms. For right now, just compile targets on 5 × 8-inch lead cards, or start a lead list on notepaper and transfer them later.

PERFORMANCE STANDARD: If you are a happily employed specialist or a highly placed executive, it is quite possible that a recruiter will be involved in your next job change. If this description fits you, you will need to work hard to identify and contact every single headhunter specializing in your niche. This could be anywhere from a dozen firms to a few hundred. The further you are away from this description (for example, unemployed generalist), the less likely that a recruiter will be involved. Most management-level candidates should be able to target at least a dozen firms, as a minimum.

(For the sake of simplicity, agencies will not be considered separately for the rest of this book. All subsequent references to contingency recruiters are understood to apply, more or less, to agencies as well.)

Watch Out!

Some unscrupulous firms prey upon hapless jobseekers, particularly insecure or lazy jobseekers. **Executive marketing firms**, also known as **retail outplacement firms**, advertise in newspapers and yellow pages from coast to coast. Some of their ads intentionally imply that they are "search" firms. They offer a free evaluation of your résumé and your candidacy to lure you in for an appointment. In this appointment you are told that you are not conducting your job search correctly at all. They tell you that they have all kinds of secret resources, and can open the hidden job market like a book. They may promise to rewrite your résumé, perform research, type and mail letters, gain access to certain companies, and even polish your shoes—for a fee, of course. They tell you that someone of your stature deserves to have "multiple job offers" before deciding on a next career move. They may even show you letters from clients who are now rich, thanks to them. Somewhere in this dog and pony show they reach into a drawer and pull out a long contract with lots of little tiny type, and then they ask you for a *big* check.

Watch out! If you read that type carefully, you will discover that *no concrete promise* is made. After you write that check, you may never see Mr. Slick again. His associate, Mr. Nobrainer, will be your "Career Coach." Your first list of "exclusive" job leads may be photocopied from the yellow pages. And that is just the beginning of your long and expensive disappointment.

In general, try to avoid any firm that requests a large lump sum for vague and ill-defined career services. *Read that contract.* Call your local Better Business Bureau before your appointment. Best of all, don't be an insecure and lazy jobseeker! Learn the process yourself, and be proactive in executing and managing your job search. Your sophistication is the best protection against unscrupulous purveyors.

There are plenty of good career services out there providing well-defined services for reasonable fees. Career counselors, résumé writers, job search coaches, interview coaches, image consultants, freelance researchers, database companies, copy centers, word processing and secretarial services are all willing to quote a specific price for a specific service, and if not . . . *caveat emptor.*

Raw Leads

In summary, you should have lead lists in four distinct categories:

- Networking leads
- Companies you know you want to contact
- Job announcements culled from newspaper "help wanted" ads and other sources
- Headhunters and agencies specializing in your area

Do not read further in this book until you have at least preliminary lists in all four categories. With few exceptions, the overwhelming amount of your effort should be on maximizing your networking and companies lists. Again, *be systematic.*

You might forgo exhaustively researching these lists until you finish this book, but then it's time to buckle down like a college student. You should be able to fill in these lists *in depth* within the first week of your search. After that, you will be constantly updating them as your search evolves and you develop new contacts or adjust the direction of your search.

CHAPTER 4

Develop Raw Leads into Specific Names to Contact

"Once you have a single lead, you can build a complete flow chart of the company."

—Norman King, Professional Sales Trainer

Converting Raw Leads into Developed Leads

You now have a hodgepodge of job leads consisting of company names, names of people you have known from all walks of life, names of recruiting firms, photocopied lists from business directories, and promising job announcements, some perhaps loudly proclaiming "No calls, please," or "Apply to box D12865 c/o this newspaper."

Your goal now is to develop every one of these, or as many as possible, into lead cards with the exact **name, title, address,** and **daytime telephone number** for a hiring authority or a direct referral source. Remember, a **hiring authority** is someone who is personally able to hire you. A **direct referral source** is someone who is personally able to refer you to a hiring authority.

As any sales pro will tell you, get the name of one executive or manager in the company and you can get the names of all the rest. From now until you are employed, all your job-search activity hinges upon your ability to identify hiring authorities and direct referral sources by name, because you cannot approach them if you don't know who they are.

In the next chapter you will learn how to make these people speak with you by telephone and meet with you in person. In this chapter, we will concentrate on methods, from the mundane to the tricky, to generate names of decision-makers.

Seven Ways to Generate Names of Decision-Makers in Companies

Methods recommended for everybody:

1. **Use standard reference materials.** This will give you names of senior officers, which is all you need to get started.

2. **Work your network for referrals.** Ask enough people and you will find somebody who knows somebody who can introduce you to the pope.

3. **Call and ask.** Obvious, perhaps, but you'd be shocked how many people don't even try it.

4. **If it's a small company, call the Better Business Bureau.** Your local Better Business Bureau will tell you the name of the owner and top officers.

5. **If it's a publicly held company, call the investor relations department.** Ask for general information on the company.

6. **Start with the CEO's office and come down, asking *secretaries*.** They'll give you names to get rid of you.

A tricky method that is interesting, but not for everybody:

7. **Any version of the "wrong number" ploy, an old sales trick**.

Depending on how aggressive you want to be, you can build a complete flow chart of almost any company starting with as little as the name on the building. Your goal is to identify hiring authorities and direct referral sources within a targeted company. In pursuit of this goal, use all six of the basic techniques *even if they make you uncomfortable.* You absolutely must treat your job search as a sales and marketing campaign, or go to the back of the line and wait patiently for any jobs left over after those who know how to look for work take their pick. These first six techniques are simply good business. (On the other hand, don't use a *"wrong number"* technique if it makes you uncomfortable.)

❋

As mentioned in the last chapter, books like *Standard & Poor's Register of Corporations, Directors, & Executives* can provide the names of senior officers. Other sources for names of officers and line managers are business and popular press articles or a company's own publicity materials (see below). Even if you're from out of town or don't know a soul in the company, you can use such resources to launch your search. (Again, see the appendix: "Resources You Can Use to Research Potential Employers.")

Data from any written resource will need to be verified by telephone. Just call the main telephone number for the company and ask something like this: "Hello. Is Bill Johnson still the V.P. of Planning & Development? And he does go by 'Bill' and not 'William'? Thank you very much. Could you put me through please?" (Don't actually contact anyone until you've read the next chapter, however, or you won't know what to say to Bill when you reach him.)

One of the best ways to get a name is from someone who knows somebody who works in one of the companies you have targeted. Be sure to carry around a list of companies you want to crack, and ask all your contacts: "Who do you know at Acme Equipment?" "Who do you know at Spacely Sprocket?" and so on. Language is very important. Your contacts will think harder and longer if you ask "Who do you know at . . ." than if you ask "Do you know anybody at . . ." In general, try to avoid any question that can be answered with a simple "yes" or "no." For more on sales language, read Walther's *Power Talking*. We'll cover networking in depth in the next section of this chapter.

Also, any time you can access a principal at a company you are interested in, you can ask him outright for a referral to someone else in the firm. Even ridiculously famous people can be quite accessible if you attend one of their lectures or meet them at a trade show or convention. Try to corner them just before or after a

PEP TALK TO SALES STAFF

"...and in closing, I'd like to leave you with two words: *or else.*"

lecture or speech, or during intermission, and get right to the point because you may have only a few seconds to convey who you are and what you want.

I have spoken with candidates who have actually joined health clubs or hung out in bars near employers where they wanted to meet someone. This approach sounds like a questionable application of zeal, but you have to admire their gumption.

❋

No matter what kind of lead you have, from a rumor to a detailed job announcement, be sure to take the trouble to call the company and ask for the name of the decision-maker you want. You should do this at least 100 percent of the time.

If the company has a full-time switchboard operator instead of a receptionist, you are in luck. Operators are trained to route calls in; receptionists are trained to screen calls out. A switchboard operator can be a gold mine of information. Try to get the targeted person's name, including correct spelling *and pronunciation,* exact title, direct dial telephone number, and work habits.

Start with the basics. "Hello. I recently read an article about your company's Cloud Scrubber project. I need to speak to the chief engineer on that, but I don't know his name. Could you help me with that?" Basically, you are just calling and asking for a person by title. Here's another script illustrating the technique: "Hi. I need to speak to the accounting manager. What's her name, please?" As an alternate approach, instead of asking for the name itself, try asking for its spelling. "I have a letter I'm trying to send to your VP of marketing. May I know the correct spelling and exact title?"

After you get a name, go on to find out as much as you can about your contact. "Does she tend to come in early or work late? Does she go by 'Carol' or 'Caroline'?

And do you know if she is in town all this week?" It's even OK to ask workstyle questions. "I'm trying to decide what to wear to a meeting. Would you say she is more of a formal or an informal person?" When quizzing an operator like this, acknowledge that she may have other calls. "I know you may have other calls you need to handle. I don't mind at all if you need to put me on hold. I'd be happy to wait. I just appreciate you taking the time to answer these questions for me." Record all this type of information directly onto your 5 × 8-inch lead cards.

A related technique is to ask for your counterpart. Zig Ziglar, the sales guru, recommends a script like this: "Hi. I'm Janet Elliassen, a director of EDP, and I need to speak with my counterpart at Children's Hospital about a problem I'm having. Who would that be?"

If the company has a receptionist who has been told to screen unsolicited calls, you may have to be a little more sophisticated. First, just try one of the direct approaches mentioned here; if that fails, use some of the other telephone techniques in this and the next chapter. Don't ever forget that operators, receptionists, secretaries, and clerks talk to the bosses more than you do, so be nice and be image-conscious in every single contact. My own office manager often prefaces calls with comments like, "This guy is a real jerk, but he insists on speaking to you," or "Could you talk to this lady? She seems really nice." You may not hear these comments, but they are common, and have tremendous impact on the reception of your message.

❋

If your target is a small company, a call to the Better Business Bureau will get you the owner's name and how long the company has been in business, at least. While you are at it, you may as well find out if they have a history of consumer complaints. Some industries are licensed or regulated by state consumer protection agencies, and these agencies will provide similar information to the public. States maintain voluminous amounts of data on everything from psychotherapy to auto repair, and it is readily accessible to the savvy jobseeker.

❋

If your target is a publicly held corporation, call and ask for the investor relations department. Tell them you are interested in investing in the company, and ask for an annual report and any information on the company they may have for general distribution. You will usually get slick publications full of photographs and names of company officers, rosy editorials on plans for the future, and reports of better-than-expected recent performance. Some companies have corporate communications departments that also have these kind of publications for general release.

If you have a regular stockbroker, enlist her help for the duration of your job search. She has more on-line information about companies than you could possibly imagine. Tell her that your ability to continue to invest with her hinges upon your success in this job search.

If you have an appointment with someone, you can call his company's public relations department and get similar information. Say something like this: "I have an appointment with someone at the company next week and I want to be informed for the meeting. Could you send me any general information brochures about Megadiversicorp?"

Be careful with PR departments, however, as some are staffed by grizzled ex-journalists with a territorial interest in protecting their employers. Before you even see it coming, you may get grilled by a professional: "Who are you? Who are you with? Why do you want to know? What do you know about us so far? How'd you find that out? . . . And you have a meeting with whom?"

Even though they often stock the same publications, investor relations and public relations departments are quite different. Anyone should feel comfortable calling investor relations, but don't call PR unless you know what you are doing.

✳

Once you get the names of top officers, secretaries can help you get the other names you want. One executive told me that he got his first real break in business when he learned how to talk to secretaries. "They answer the phone, they're friendly, and nine times out of ten they'll give you the information you need without your having to talk to some inaccessible bigshot."

To get to the executive suite, all you have to do is ask. For example, if you know that the CEO's name is E. E. Loader, you can start at the main switchboard, "I need to speak to E. E. Loader's secretary, but before you put me through, may I know his or her name please?" Then, when you get through, put in a more-or-less direct request for the information you want. "Hello. Sorry to bother you. I don't think I really need to speak to Mr. Loader. I was just trying to find out who is in charge of training and development and they put me through to you." Again, be sure to follow up with "How do you spell that?" and your other inquiries. End with "Can you put me through or should I go back to the main switchboard?"

Of course, you can call any executive's secretary and use this technique. If you don't succeed with the first one, just call another. There's a hidden advantage to this secretarial referral system, and it comes into play when you try to penetrate gatekeepers' screens. As one sales pro told me, "The secretary of the EVP is intimidated by the secretary of the CEO, and so on right down the line. No matter what happens with your first call, you can call the next one down and say 'I was just talking to Rosalyn, and she suggested that I speak with *your* boss.'" Of course, you want to get "Rosalyn" to make such a referral. With this kind of intro, you are bound to get through.

Whenever you are calling an executive with a private secretary, always find out that secretary's name at the earliest opportunity. Ask whoever is forwarding your call, or ask the secretary outright, "May I know *your* name please?" Often, you will get more cooperation all around by asking for a secretary in the first place, rather than asking for the executive.

✸

The "wrong number" ploy is more questionable that the above techniques, but is indisputably effective. There are several versions, two of which we will cover here. Anytime you can get the information you need in a more straightforward manner, you should do so. However, if you find yourself "stopped at the gate" with other techniques, then consider trying one of these strategies.

One version is to get past the front desk by asking for some department that every company has, for example, accounts receivable. Then, once you are patched through: "Did you say 'accounts receivable'? I was trying to reach the person in charge of benefits administration. Oh, you can patch me through? Great! Before you do maybe you can help me out with something. I'm embarrassed to admit it, but I don't even know whom to ask for over there. . . Can you spell that for me?"

The other version is to dial intentionally into a wrong number. In short, if you can't get past the front desk, dial around it. If the main telephone number is 555-1600, call 555-1601, 555-1602, 555-1603, 555-1604, 555-1605, 555-1606, and so on, until you reach someone who can help you out. All you need is the name of one department manager, and you are in business.

✸

Obviously none of these techniques will work 100 percent of the time, but all of them will work some of the time. You can use all these techniques on the same company, but not, of course, all in the same day. Do this sort of background research all the time on a large number of companies, but only a little at a time on any individual company. If you call the same company several times in the same day, the receptionist is going to start recognizing your voice. If you use the trickier techniques, sometimes it's even a good idea to trade this research role with another jobseeker, swapping leads one-for-one in two totally different areas. This solves the voice recognition problem.

What is your immediate goal here? To obtain the names of hiring authorities, people who have the power and the position to hire you into your next job. You must have the names of hiring authorities in order to approach them using the techniques presented in the next chapter. In the previous chapter, this one, and the next, you are getting one of the most aggressive job-search strategies ever presented to the general public. Once you see the total picture—how these intensive search techniques work together—you will realize that you don't need to know a soul to succeed in your job search. Connections can help you tremendously, but they are in no way required for this type of search. You can be dropped out of an airplane into a new state with no friends or connections whatsoever, and still design, launch, and succeed in an aggressive job-search campaign.

In every facet of your search, remember these three tenets:

○ **No technique works 100 percent of the time.**

○ **No one application or rejection should define your job search.**

○ **Your goal is to improve your odds on *every* application.**

There are no guarantees. *You are striving to improve your odds of getting job offers in return for your job-search effort.* That's all. You will get better and better at getting names, accessing decision-makers, and getting appointments for meetings as you continue your search.

How to Make Your Network Work for You

In the last chapter we discussed how fortuitous even the most accidental networking connections can be. In this section we are going to discuss how to be absolutely systematic in utilizing your network, how to work your network, and how to make your network work for you.

Now is the time to call up everyone on your networking lists and let her know that you are on the market, exactly what types of jobs you are interested in, and what she can do for you. Some older workers are reluctant to let anyone know they need a new job. They entered the work force when there was still a stigma to unemployment. Their reticence to broadcast their job search costs them weeks of additional unemployment. Don't let this happen to you.

A job search is like an advertising campaign: You want exposure for your product. Becoming agoraphobic, retreating into depression, or otherwise giving in to some imagined stigma because you need a new position can be highly counterproductive to a proper job search. The old image of the unemployed as social pariah is nearly dead, and the sooner it passes on the better. In large part due to the waves of economic restructuring that began over a decade ago, needing a job is an unfortunate but expected and common occurrence. It's about as shameful as needing a new car. It happens to everybody sooner or later.

Some years ago I had a client from Silicon Valley who had been a key member of so many skyrocketing start-ups he probably knew half the unlisted phone numbers in the area. He jumped from one opportunity to the next without missing a day's work. But when he found himself without a job for the first time in many years, he retreated into his house, lost touch with all his contacts, and began to look for work *in secret.* The really remarkable thing about this story is that his entire background was in marketing and sales.

When he described his process of responding to newspaper ads and waiting for replies, I realized he needed a complete overhaul of his job-search strategy. Once he understood the material you are receiving in this book, he went home, dusted off his address book, and started to advertise his product. He found a consulting contract within a week, and a new career position shortly thereafter.

✳

You must be *systematic* and *comprehensive* in working your network. Your goal is to contact every single person on your networking lists at least once, and then pick a core group of contacts whom you will contact regularly until you are employed again. Before you can begin, you need to know two things: what your objective is, and what you want your networking lead to do for you.

Fill in the blanks in this sentence: "I'm interested in positions in _____, but I am also exploring opportunities in _____." In general, try to narrow your search down to one or two areas only. Don't confuse your contacts with a laundry list of divergent interests.

Then, divide your contacts into three categories: **hiring authorities** (those able to hire you if they needed you), **direct referral sources** (those able to refer you to hiring authorities), and **indirect referral sources** (everybody else in the world).

Indirect referral sources are the easiest. Just mail them a copy of your résumé with a short note informing them of your search and asking them to ring you if they have any **ideas**, **leads**, or **referrals** for you. (See the frontispiece for notepaper specifications and other items you should have in your "job-search supply cabinet.") Be sure to advise them as to whether you are looking confidentially or whether they can discuss your search with anyone. The notes can be handwritten or typewritten. They do not have to be perfect, and you certainly should not let this part of your search stall the overall project. Be sure to include your business card or a "jobseeker" card. Here are two notes such as you might send:

Dear Ted:

After a couple of years with Dewey, Cheatham, and Howe, I have decided to explore opportunities with other firms. I am interested in specializing in estate planning and probate, but I am also exploring some opportunities to serve as house counsel to a pension fund, a major trust, or a foundation. I'd be interested in hearing any ideas you might have for a JD/CPA. As you might imagine, I need you to keep this totally confidential at this stage.

I appreciate any help you can offer me.

Your old roommate,
Bill S. Preston, Esq.
Enclosures

> Dear Sis,
>
> I guess mother told you the news about The Bazaar. Anyway, I will be looking rather intensively for a retail position in Boston. If you know anybody in retail you could introduce me to, I'd appreciate it. I'll be in town for a week at the first of the month.
>
> Yours,
> Dorothy
> PS: I've enclosed a few copies of my résumé. Feel free to forward them along to anybody you can think of. Thanks.

You can write your own notes to suit your personality, the nature of your contact, and your resources. After sending out a few hundred of these, be prepared for an onslaught of bad advice. People will call you up and try to convince you that you want to get involved in selling franchises for Christian dating services or mowing lawns to earn a little money to tide you over. You must accept this type of advice with grace, and say, "That's an interesting idea, Uncle Bud. I'll keep that in mind, but I really want to focus my search on _____ right now. If you hear anything about _____, you be sure to give me a call."

But mixed in with that bad advice will be real leads. "I heard that Bridget's tennis partner is in some kind of high tech marketing. Why don't you give her a call?" "You know, I just realized today that I know a guy at the office who used to manage production scheduling for that Black Belt Tires company you asked about. He said he still knows everybody over there. He said for you to give him a call. You want his number?"

Direct referral sources will be people in the same industry as you, or people with family members or other direct connections to the industry you have chosen. **Hiring authorities** most certainly work in the industry you have targeted. Most of your networking effort should be devoted to direct referral sources and hiring authorities.

Every single one of these people must be called at least twice. Before or after the first call, you need to write them a note or a more formal letter and send them your résumé, but the most important thing for you to do is to call them back after they have had a few days to think about your job search.

Make it clear in your contacts that you are not asking these people for a job. You want them to keep their eyes and ears open on your behalf, and forward along any **ideas**, **leads**, or **referrals** they think of. You are literally extending your network as far as it will go. Like axons stretching out to incredible distances in all directions from a brain cell, your network collects and forwards job leads, ideas, rumors, and other job-related information to you.

Incidentally, if you have the lead time, the most graceful way to manage your network is to contact everyone on it for some other reason a few months before you begin your job search. You should do this periodically anyway. People on your networking lists should hear from you from time to time, not just once every two to ten years when you need their help with a job search.

I have an acquaintance who is a Hollywood business type, a consummate schmoozer, a man who makes his living on the quality of his wits and his connections. He makes a point of communicating with everyone on his network at least twice a year. Some of these people he hasn't seen in forever, but he stays in contact with them faithfully. "You never know," he says. "Maybe in the next movie I'll have to find a snake handler, or a trick cowboy who speaks Japanese, or someone who can tell me how an electron microscope actually works from the electron's point of view. There are people I could call right now on practically any project."

Remember, you want **ideas**, **leads**, and **referrals** not just once, but for the duration of your job search. For direct referral sources and hiring authorities on your networking lists, you can use notes similar to the examples above or a more formal cover letter such as the following one. Note that even in contacting a hiring authority, *the candidate may choose not to ask for a job.* He doesn't need to. If the hiring authority has an opening and sees a fit, she'll bring it up herself.

Dear Ms. Cartel:

We haven't spoken in awhile so I've forwarded a résumé to update you on my recent activities. I've left Halsey-Waters and taken a short sabbatical on the West Coast. I will be returning to Chicago soon, however, and I will be seeking a position.

Since you know the quality of my work, would you take a moment and consider who might be interested? My interest is a position as art director or project manager over major direct response projects, but I would not be adverse to any good opportunity. I'll be calling you soon to see if you have any suggestions. In the meantime, my best wishes as always.

Thanks for your help.

Sincerely,
C. Bart Holloway
Enclosure.

Whether you write first and then call, or call first and then write, that first call to a networking contact should be thorough. Most networking calls run something like this: "Janet, do you know anybody who could help me out in my job search?" "No, Bob, nothing comes to mind." "Well, thanks. If you hear anything, let me know."

"Sure, Bob. I will." *And that's it.* Janet goes on with her day, and by five o'clock she has forgotten about Bob and his job search entirely.

Don't ask something vague and then just hang up when they say "nothing comes to mind." Have a whole series of fairly specific questions ready.

- What ideas, leads, or referrals do you have for me?
- Who do you know in your company who might be interested in someone like me?
- Does your company have an executive telephone book? Can you get your hands on one for me?
- Who do you know in another company who might need someone like me?
- Who do you know in another division or branch of your company who might need someone with my skills?
- What related industries can you think of that use these same skills?
- Who do you know in that related industry?
- I've also been thinking about some other areas myself. Who do you know in the computer software industry? Who do you know in biotech? Who do you know in _____?
- I also have a short list of companies I'm trying to crack. Who do you know at Vox Nova? Who do you know at Amalgamated Diversified? Who do you know at Potluck Catering? Who do you know at _____?
- What about people you might know outside of business? Who do you know in your church who might be able to refer me to someone in these areas? Who do you know from your health club who might know someone in these companies or industries?

Then, tell them *exactly* when you'll call back. "You've been a great help, Janet. These leads look very promising. I'll let you know if anything comes out of this. Listen, I want you to keep your eyes and ears open for me. Are you going to be in town next week? Great. I'll call you on Friday to see if you've heard anything new or thought of anything else. I really appreciate this, and if I can ever return the favor, you can be sure I will."

You may even want to say something like this: "Janet, you just know so many people in this business. Would you mind if I called you once every week or two until I land a job? You're bound to hear something on the grapevine sooner or later. Listen, if you don't have any new leads, you don't even need to take the call. I'll just leave a message and if you don't ring back I'll know it's because you haven't heard anything. I don't want to inconvenience you."

You absolutely must follow through on even the most casual of commitments to your networking contacts. If you say you'll call on Friday or once every ten days, be sure you do. If your networking contacts decide you are too flaky, they won't help you any more. Mark your 5 × 8-inch lead card for the date of next activity: "Call Janet this Friday." Then drop her card in with the others that you have scheduled for action on Friday.

You can also approach any hiring authority or direct referral source using the techniques in the next chapter.

Creating a Network from Scratch

Most candidates who don't think they have a network haven't bothered to sit down and make the lists you made in the last chapter. Some may start with a meager network, or a network full of people who know nothing about their targeted field, but very few will have no network at all.

You will enhance, augment, and refine your network as your search progresses. Even if you don't know a soul, you can create a network from scratch. Don't forget that everyone you meet for the duration of your search becomes part of your network. Every meeting you arrange will bring *at least* one new person into your network. If you are not a contender for a known opening, never leave a meeting without saying "I'll give you a ring in a week to see if you have any leads or ideas for me." (If you are a candidate for a known opening, don't seek referrals. Doing so reveals one of two things: either you lack confidence in your candidacy, or don't want the position you are applying for.)

Finally, if you are a reasonably polite person you can invite people who don't know you yet to help you. Use any form of research to get the names of players in your targeted industry, then write a series of letters like this:

Dear Mr. Clark:

As someone new in the area, I am interested in circulating around to meet players in the industry here in L.A. If you would do me the favor of a brief meeting to discuss my background and refer me to individuals or companies that might be interested, I would greatly appreciate it.

I've enclosed a copy of my résumé for your review. My strengths are listed clearly, and I would be happy to expand on any detail. You're probably in New York for market week, so I'll call you the middle of next week once you've had a chance to catch your breath, say Wednesday or Thursday.

I'm looking forward to our conversation, and if there is any lead or resource I can provide for you, I would be more than happy to do so.

Thanks again, and I look forward to speaking with you soon.

Yours sincerely,
K. T. Swain
Enclosure.

How to Get a Name for Announced Openings

As mentioned repeatedly, pursuing announced openings is not the best way to look for a new job. First of all, you are entering the search with scads of other candidates who are too lazy to do job development. Job development is approaching prospective employers and trying to sell them your skills *before* they design and advertise a job. Job development is proactive. Responding to announced openings is reactive.

Once a job has been defined and announced, you have to measure up to the vision of the ideal candidate in the employer's mind. Perhaps you have seen those ads in the paper for someone with ten years of experience, a recent master's degree, and a documented miracle witnessed by at least one hundred people. Then the ad goes on to offer virtually entry-level wages! That's an ad written by an employer who has made up in his mind an ideal candidate.

During the time after the employer knows he has a problem and before he defines one of these ideal candidates as the solution to it, he can be quite receptive to a self-promoted candidacy. The same employer who would have welcomed the opportunity to avoid an expensive, time-consuming search, will not abandon it once it gets started.

This imaginary ideal candidate is only the half of it. The other side of the problem is the competition. Somewhere out there there is someone closer to that ideal than you. Someone who is cheaper, faster, better, more experienced, smarter (or dumber) than you. Announced openings draw dozens, hundreds, and even thousands of candidates for every opening. So you not only have to measure up to the ideal candidate, you have to compete with lots of other, very real, candidates.

In spite of all this, many candidates do find employment by responding to announced openings. For every single announced opening you decide to pursue, you will greatly increase your odds if you develop it *just like any other job lead.* Use the techniques in this chapter to turn such a raw lead into a developed lead, complete with the name, title, address, and daytime telephone number for the decision-maker. Then pursue that decision-maker as if the ad didn't exist.

WARNING: Some companies use fake names for the contact person for announced openings as a way of screening calls and mail. You can use the methods in this chapter to find out the names of real line managers, and then apply to them directly.

Even if the ad says no calls, call anyway. "I heard your company is looking for a _____. How would I apply for that job? To whom should I address my cover letter? What kind of skills and experience are you looking for? How soon do you expect to make the placement?" and so on, just like any other job lead. Some savvy candidates trade "no calls" ads with a person of the opposite sex, so no matter how bad the call bombs, the candidacy is undamaged.

When looking for work out of town, your chances of obtaining a placement through newspaper ads depends on your level. If you are a national property, that is, a candidate the company would happily relocate in order to recruit, then your chances are good. If you are a middle manager, you will need to volunteer to relocate and even to travel to interviews at your own expense, or you will lose out every single time to local talent. Be sure your cover letter mentions how much you are looking forward to returning or going to the beautiful weather and people of the great state of _____. Some middle- and lower-level candidates have had great luck by putting a local address on their résumé and letters. For more on this technique, see my book, *The Overnight Résumé*.

Blind box ads tend to bollix jobseekers. "Blind box ads" are help wanted ads that do not identify the advertiser. The candidate is instructed to apply to a post office box or a box number in care of the newspaper the ad appears in. Employers run blind box ads for several perfectly good reasons: they may not want their own employees to know of impending staff changes, they may not want their competitors to guess their business plans based on the types of positions they are recruiting, or they may not want their customers to worry about management changes until they are *faits accomplis*. Other advantages to the employer are that they do not have to acknowledge applications or otherwise trouble themselves with the public relations aspects of a recruiting effort.

Some candidates eschew blind ads, but the only cost of applying to these ads is the cost of the stamp for the envelope, and the only risk—if you are still employed—is that you might apply to your own employer. Still, whenever you can, you should try to develop these leads just like any other job lead.

First of all, some "blind ads" actually list a street address but not the company. (Would that make them "visually impaired ads"?) Either drive by that address or go to the library and ask for a reverse directory to discover the advertiser. Reverse directories are like telephone books, but instead of looking up names, you can look up addresses. Once you get the name of the company, you can discover the decision-maker without much further ado; then approach the company like any other job lead.

If the ad lists a post office box, march into the nearest post office with the advertisement and say, "According to USPS Communication 352.44 'Disclosure of Names and Addresses of Customers,' Paragraph 4, 'Post office box address,' Section 1, 'Business use,' you are required to provide me with the name, address, and telephone number of this advertiser. To quote 352.44e(1): 'The recorded name, address, and telephone number of the holder of a post office box being used for the purpose of doing or soliciting business with the public . . . will be furnished to any person.'" The local postmaster must comply with this regulation whether the box in question is physically at that station or not, and whether the box in question was actually rented by a business or an individual.

Only when the ad lists a newspaper box number is it truly "blind." If you are afraid that the advertiser is your own employer (or any other employer you do not wish to contact), just prepare your application and seal it in one envelope addressed to the box number. Then place that application inside a second envelope addressed to the newspaper's mailroom, and enclose a letter such as this:

Dear Daily Truth:

I am responding to help wanted advertising Box 3128 from Sunday's paper, 3/14/93. Please DO NOT FORWARD the enclosed application if the employer is Smith Linoleum or Floors-to-Roll. Thank you for your diligence in this matter.

You should note that with the proliferation of search firms and consultants in management-level employment, you can never be entirely sure you are not inadvertently applying to your own employer. Personnel consultants often run ads that do not reveal their client. Any company could be hiding behind an ad placed by "Smelte, Kline & Gubanski." As a matter of established professional ethics, a search or screening firm is not supposed to reveal to an employer that they have received an application from within the employer's own ranks, but this is not one of the ethics that these firms feel most strongly about.

If the ad gives you enough information to guess the nature of the employer's business, then you have a great job lead. Apply to the blind box, of course, but then pick up the phone and call the human resources department of all the employers you can think of that might be behind that particular ad. This is one of the few times you will actually contact a human resources department in an aggressive job search. Job orders originate with line managers. Most HR departments are reactive, and without an existing job order they will not forward your information to line managers no matter how impressive your background. Except for handling announced openings, most HR departments function to screen applicants out and thwart their job-search efforts.

In the case of blind box ads, however, you have nothing to lose. Just call them up and say, "Hello. My name is Angel Kelly, and I heard your company was looking for a _____. Who would I talk to about this opening?" You may find the company that placed the ad, and also you may get lucky and find some other company that wants to talk to you anyway.

Finally, in applying to any type of blind or screened ad, you can use a screen of your own. This technique is best illustrated in the following response letter. Note that the letter is enticing, but just vague enough that it would be difficult to trace back to the principal:

Dear Advertiser:

A friend has asked me to write on her behalf concerning the position you have advertised. She is eminently qualified for this opportunity. Some of her accomplishments relative to your requirements are as follows:

- Directed sales and marketing for a start-up medical equipment manufacturing company using the same technologies mentioned in your advertisement. Facilitated the migration from R&D to full commercialization. Brought a market focus to what had been an engineering-driven company. Launched product, exceeded goals for gross and net revenues, current direct sales in range of $15 to $25 million.
- Created distributor and product support networks in other regions of the United States, effectively doubling gross sales with minimal increase in fixed expenses.
- Strong technical background. Advanced degree in applied physics, undergraduate degree in mathematics, minor in business. Effective bridge between engineering and sales.

Due to my friend's prominent and critical position with her current employer, I have been asked to serve as her proxy. I am not a placement professional; I am providing this service as a professional courtesy to you both.

Please call me to arrange a confidential interview.

Sincerely,

Whata Friend

Of course, the potential employer must reveal its identity before your friend reveals yours. This is perhaps a long-shot approach, but if you want to protect yourself, there is no other way.

How to Approach Headhunters

In the last chapter you identified headhunters who specialize in your function and industry. As mentioned there, headhunters are not a particularly fruitful source if you need a job *now*. Nevertheless, no management-level search would be complete without checking in with at least a dozen of them.

First, call the firm, tell them who you are and what you want, and ask them exactly which consultant would have the most expertise in your particular area. Just as with your target companies, discover and write to a person, not a firm, and you must be able to specify what type of job you are interested in. In all aspects of your search, you should be able to give a statement as short and precise as the following:

I am a development officer with nine years of experience. My last position was assistant director of development for a hospital foundation, where I was also managing director of a $20 million capital campaign. I am interested in positions as assistant director of development in an arts organization, a hospital or other medi-

> *cal foundation, or perhaps a private college. Because of the strength of my back-*
> *ground, I would also be qualified to be director of development for a smaller orga-*
> *nization with $1 to $3 million annual fundraising requirements. My background*
> *spans personal giving, events, direct response, database administration, statisti-*
> *cal analysis, and close coordination with affiliated volunteer organizations.*

Once you get the name of a specific consultant, write her a letter and enclose your résumé. In your letter, you want to convey that you understand how headhunters work, and that you are a savvy jobseeker. Refer to the headhunter's clients in clauses like "timely introduction to one of your clients," or "I should think that one of your clients would be quite interested in someone who has built a European sales organization from scratch." To reassure the headhunter that you will not embarrass her, use statements like this: "I know I can make a compelling presentation of my candidacy."

Most important of all, it is absolutely critical that you include the following statement: "Of course it is understood that you would not forward my résumé to any potential employer without discussing the specific opportunity with me first."

This clause keeps the headhunter from "floating" your résumé to every employer in his client base, the same employers you may be trying to develop on your own. This little clause could save your next employer one-third of your annual salary, and it could save you a job offer. If the employer gets your résumé from the headhunter first, *even if you develop a job offer separately and entirely on your own,* there's a price on your head. The headhunter is entitled to pursue his fee. Just to be fair, few headhunters today engage in this practice of floating résumés, but you don't want to find out about this the hard way.

You can state your salary interests to a headhunter, but you don't have to. Try to make it a range from the absolute least you'd accept or your current salary, whichever is lower, to a little more than you think is a reasonable expectation in this career move. Listing your motivation for seeking a career move is also optional, and should always be put in a positive light.

Here is a typical letter introducing a candidate to a headhunter:

Dear Ms. Placement:

I have 18 years of increasing responsibility as a sales rep and sales manager in the food-service industry. If you have any clients seeking someone with this type of background, perhaps you will find these accomplishments pertinent:

- Increased volume by 117% for an established company. This was the result of a revitalization of sales efforts. No gimmicks—just hard, smart work.

- Introduced new product to 30,000 lbs. in sales in first 90 days, more than 15 times our original target.
- Established sales programs for a new company resulting in 15,000 cases sold in first eight months.
- Earned <u>National</u> Salesman of the Year award in second year with McCormick & Company, a major national company.
- Trained in sales and marketing with Proctor & Gamble.

The above shows a top performer. For additional detail, I have provided the attached résumé for your review. My present company is very happy with my performance, but it has gone through two mergers in the last six months. My position certainly seems to be secure, but I feel it is time for a wise man to consider his options.

My salary target is something in the $60K to $80K range. If you have anything of interest to discuss, call me at your earliest opportunity. Otherwise, I will ring you to follow up in about ten days to introduce myself personally and answer any questions you may have.

Of course, it is understood that you would not forward my résumé to any potential employer without discussing the specific opportunity with me first.

I look forward to speaking with you soon.

Sincerely,
A. Strong Candidate
Enclosure

Always call recruiters to follow up on your mailings. Some don't like it, but don't worry, they'll let you know if they don't want to speak with you. Try to select about a dozen recruiters whom you call back every couple of weeks for the duration of your job search. Treat them just like prime networking contacts.

❋

A problem with some recruiters is that they will try to ram a square peg into a round hole. Do not let a recruiter take over your job search, or you may find yourself squirming in a bad fit. Also, some recruiters will eat up a lot of your time on wild goose chases, if you let them. Your time costs them nothing, after all. Let the headhunter know your job specifications, and stick to them.

Always interrogate headhunters about any opportunity being dangled in your face. "What are the responsibilities and challenges facing the next incumbent? Tell me more about the product line and the technologies involved. To whom does this position report? What type of company is it? How much business travel is involved? Would I need to relocate? What salary range are we talking about here? What happened to the last person in this position? What skills, experience, or character traits has the employer identified as most critical for this placement?"

Only if the job is of genuine interest to you should you pursue it. Otherwise, level with the recruiter. "Well, Cheryl, this sounds interesting but it's not quite right for me. I told you I have young children, and I can't accept a position with more than a little travel. I tell you what, though—I have an acquaintance who would be perfect for this. I'll give you her name, and I'll let her know you might give her a ring. I appreciate the call, and do please call me again when you have something that's up my alley."

Confidentiality & Time Management for All This if You Are Still Employed

The most successful careerists never really *stop* looking for work. They update their résumés sometime during their first ninety days on a new job. They have a large network, and they are responsive to the leads that come in over the wires. Even if they are happy, they answer headhunters' calls, they check out rumors, and they pay attention. Some of them even read the want ads every Sunday as a sort of hobby.

These people don't necessarily change companies every six months, but they know the market and they have a sense of their worth on that market. Many of them use these same search techniques within their own companies. They monitor openings, keep tabs on other departments and divisions, and find reasons to have informational interviews across organizational lines.

One of the most diligent careerists I know has been with the same employer for over a decade, but she has maneuvered and positioned herself for a remarkable series of promotions using these techniques. "I knew I could leave at any time, so I guess it made me more fearless within the organization," she told me.

Incidentally, one of the most important factors for getting a promotion or a transfer is timing. You need to have your current projects draw to a close just as the organization needs to launch the projects under your targeted position. Monitoring the timing of projects all across the organization is one way to enhance your ability to engineer your own promotions and transfers. This is a little-understood aspect of the nexus between individual career needs and organizational needs: In many cases, a promotion may not be a reward for service, but simply a reward for being available.

All this being said, however, how do you find the time for all this if you are currently employed? The answer is simple: **You make it.**

Of paramount importance: You absolutely must find time to make all these phone calls. Better to have a few applications that you manage intensively than many that you manage poorly. If you regularly work a forty-six-hour week, be careful that you don't suddenly change all your work habits, or you may as well hang a neon sign around your neck, "Looking for a New Job."

Some candidates casually mention at work that their last dentist visit was a disaster, and they have to have a whole series of appointments. Then they set those "appointments" well in advance and keep them. Others tell their employers that they have some personal, family, accounting, or legal problems that they will have to spend some time on the phone trying to get resolved. In any case, before making job-search calls, be sure to shut your door firmly.

If you are honest to the core, as many people are, start having lunch with a friend fairly often. Have her show up at the office to pick you up. She can sit and enjoy a fine meal while you spend the hour on the restaurant's pay phone.

Some jobseekers take vacation days or personal business days. Some run down the stairs on every break to use a pay phone on another floor. It doesn't matter what you do, as long as you do it. On the other hand, don't let your work performance fall off noticeably or you may find your time problem resolved for you.

If you are not sure that you are going to leave, *don't tell a soul at the office.* Everybody will know about it within two days if you do. If you are absolutely sure you want to leave, consider leveling with your boss. It's a modern world. Some companies are quite understanding and cooperative, and they might appreciate the opportunity to plan for your departure. Other companies will fire you on the spot.

Develop Some Leads NOW

Before you go on to the next chapter, look over your piles of lead cards. Test out at least a few techniques to find names of decision-makers. You want **name**, **correct spelling**, **title**, **address**, and **daytime phone number.** Remember, you will not succeed in 100 percent of your attempts *and you should not expect to.* You are simply trying to increase your odds. Every call you make reduces your tenure as a jobseeker. Every lead you develop is a lead that is much more likely to be fruitful than the leads you cannot develop.

You can go on to the next chapter without working *all* your raw leads into developed leads, because it can be a real advantage to be ready to push all the way through to your targeted decision-maker on the first call. However, do not simply read this book, take a few notes, nod your head and say, "That's interesting." Get up off your chair and run an aggressive, intensive campaign. Don't bother to read further until you've made that commitment and are ready to live up to it.

There are those lead cards, waiting to be developed . . .

CHAPTER 5

Turn a Name into an Appointment

"If the personnel people are doing their jobs, namely screening applications, the chances are very good that you will never get to see the person who has the power to hire you."
—Rogers, Johnson, Alexander and Schmitz,
Secrets of the Hidden Job Market

Telephone Power

Some people have a talent for telephone communication and some do not, but anybody can do it. Some years ago a young man came into my office for advice. He looked so weary and forlorn that his head actually hung down.

Something was wrong with his telephone technique. "I used to be so good at this," he said. "I used to be able to reach any decision-maker in California real estate. Just pick up the phone and call them. Now that I'm looking for a job, I can't seem to reach anybody. I can't seem to get past the front desk . . . nobody returns my calls . . ."

"Who were you calling before?" I asked. "Maybe the people you are calling now require a different technique."

"I'm calling exactly the same people. I used to be so good at this," he repeated, his voice trailing off.

"Well, who were you working for before?" I asked.

"I was acquisitions representative for a consortium of Japanese real estate investors. I cataloged and priced developed properties and parcels of raw land."

When he said this, I almost choked keeping down a laugh. This kid was calling real estate tycoons and saying, "Hi, I represent a consortium of Japanese real estate investors and we'd like to tour some of your properties for possible acquisition." Can't you just see these people scrambling to return his phone calls? This was practically his first job out of college, and he got in his mind that he just had a special way with people.

You're good on the telephone when you can reach people who don't know you and can't imagine why they should take time out of their busy day to talk to you. You *can* be good on the telephone. Half of it is simply persistence, and the other half is for-mula. In this chapter we'll cover the formula; the persistence is up to you.

Now that you have the names and phone numbers for most of your contacts, you are ready to implement a full-scale **telemarketing campaign**. First, you need some basic resources. If you can afford it, you might want to have two telephone lines for the duration of your job search, one for outgoing calls, the other for incoming. If feasible, you never want any caller to get a busy signal. One candidate I worked with actually contracted for an "800" line for incoming calls for the duration of his job search.

On your incoming line you want a professional message, with your first and last name, and no screaming kids or music in the background. If your family or room-mates won't put up with this, tell them if you don't get the right job soon you're going to go crazy and they'll have to support you. Here is one of the most successful mes-sages I have ever heard: "Hello, this is David Harding. I'm in the office today, but I'm either on the other line, or I've just stepped out for a moment. Leave a message and I'll call you right back."

Whether you are home or not, check your messages several times every day, espe-cially at 11:15 A.M. and 4:15 P.M. so you can return any incoming calls before lunch and before the close of the business day.

PERFORMANCE STANDARD: Return every single phone message the same day you get it.

Make outgoing calls as early in the day as possible, starting no later than 8:00 A.M. A good schedule is to make new outgoing calls from 8:00 to 11:00 A.M., then return the morning's incoming calls promptly after 11:00. Make new outgoing calls again from 2:00 to 4:00 P.M., stopping promptly at 4:00 to return the afternoon's incoming calls. (This can get complicated if your contacts are spread across two or three time zones.) Do not place new outgoing telephone calls on Friday afternoon. Although this should be your telemarketing routine, there are plenty of reasons to break that rou-tine, as we shall see in a moment.

In general, the jobseeker's workweek is Sunday afternoon through Friday noon. Track your hours; your target is 40+ hours per week, including telemarketing, library and field research, letter and résumé writing, and focused media reading. Focused media reading does not mean lounging around with the newspaper for hours, but skimming articles for leads, flash reading want ads in your field, and devouring new career books (*without* reading every single word). We'll return to this topic in chapter 8, "Track and Troubleshoot Your Job Search."

The first obstacles you are going to run into in your telemarketing campaign are gatekeepers. Like the three-headed watchdogs guarding the gates of hell, they stand

at the gates of commerce to keep you out. With a little strategy and a little practice, however, you can get past gatekeepers as easily as if you represented a consortium of Japanese real estate investors.

Nine Ways to Get Past Gatekeepers

Methods recommended for everybody:

1. **Call and ask.** Once again, most candidates never even try, and those who do don't try enough times.

2. **Call early, late, and during lunch.** Avoid the obstructionist altogether.

3. **Use the "presumptive call" technique.** Use manner and tone of voice to establish that you are somebody who should be put through.

4. **Get referred down from a higher office.** When the call is sanctioned by a higher executive *or her secretary,* this is very effective.

5. **Ask the gatekeeper for her help.** This is a fascinating technique, a last-ditch effort, and it is usually either surprisingly effective or ends your chances.

6. **Mail something to the person you're trying to reach, stating that you will be calling.** This makes every call a "warm call."

7. **Make an appointment for the telephone call.** Schedule it just like a meeting.

8. **Cite your referral source.** Even if the gatekeeper doesn't know the referral source, you have more authority.

A tricky method that is interesting, but not for everybody:

9. **Use the "implied referral" technique, an old sales trick.**

Getting past gatekeepers takes a little practice. How many times in your business career have you heard lines like the following? "She's not available right now. Would you like to leave a message?" How many times would you call back if your contact never returned your call?

Call at least once per day for at least seven business days before abandoning a lead.

This is not a social call! This is an unsolicited business telephone call. If your social contacts don't return your phone calls, you are justified in dropping them off your social calendar. However, in the world of business, an unsolicited telephone call is a very low priority. Never take it personally when somebody does not return your calls. It is often the case that your contact *wants to talk to you*, but just hasn't yet found the time to return your call. He may be eager to speak with you, and still not call you for days and days. Help him out by calling him over and over again.

Stop calling only when you reach your targeted lead, or someone tells you "never call here again." As long as you are polite as well as persistent, you really have nothing to lose. As an old salesman once told me, "Either the guy writes me a check or he throws me out of his office. There is no other possible outcome to a sales call."

Most candidates who are otherwise savvy do not realize how many times they must attempt to complete an unsolicited business contact. Some of the salespeople I have spoken with said ten attempts is their *minimum* before they give up. In the job-search context, seven is certainly a minimum, but you may choose to adopt a higher standard. You might even consider calling twice a day, once in the morning and once in the afternoon, until you reach your intended party.

What you have to realize is that even if you never get through the gatekeeper's screen you can make an impression and influence your targeted decision-maker. You are revealing something about your tenacity and dedication with every call.

I know a stockbroker who calls a few high-profile contacts every single morning and leaves a simple message. He seldom if ever succeeds in reaching VIP targets early in his efforts to develop them as clients. He calls every day for weeks, saying something like this: "This is Clinton Wallace with Oglethorpe & Co. Have him give me a call back. My number is 212-555-1234." He always calls *at exactly the same time* to establish that he is reliable. Then, after a week or two of this, he adds a simple message: "Watch Amalgamated Diversified." He doesn't call any more. If Amalgamated Diversified ever goes up, he starts calling and leaving messages again. "Tell him I'm the guy who said to watch Amalgamated Diversified. Tell him it's up $2\frac{1}{8}$. Clinton Wallace, 212-555-1234." Then he goes back to his original cycle, "This is Clinton Wallace with Oglethorpe & Co. Have him give me a call back. My number is 212-555-1234." If he doesn't get through, in a week or so he says, "Watch Megadiversicorp." Then if Megadiversicorp ever goes up . . .

This guy cracks top accounts with no more sophisticated an approach than this. Patience and persistence are his heralds, and they serve him well. Remember, no technique works 100 percent of the time, and no one application or rejection should define your job search. You are just trying to improve your overall odds. Just as with this stockbroker, if one of your contacts doesn't work out, another one will.

Persistence is the number one way to reach your targeted contact, and it requires no sales skill whatsoever. Just remember to be courteous to those gatekeepers on every call, and keep trying.

If you suspect a particular gatekeeper is screening you out, call early, call late, and call during lunchtime. You may have better luck with the relief gatekeeper. Also, by calling early and late you will often be able to circumvent the gatekeeping cadre altogether. Middle managers and even executives often answer the phones off hours. They are very unlikely to screen your call. If they are not the party you are trying to reach, they usually put you straight through. You can combine this technique with the technique from the last chapter of calling around the main switchboard (555-1601, 555-1602, 555-1603 . . .).

One candidate I know called in the middle of the night, around 3:00 A.M. After about twenty rings he reached a security guard who told him, "Mr. Smith's not here now. He usually comes in at around six o'clock in the morning." The candidate started calling every day at 6:10, rightfully guessing that no secretaries would be at work that early. For four days he left a message on Mr. Smith's voicemail. On the fifth day Mr. Smith picked up and said, "You're right on time. What can I do for you?"

✺

It is hard to learn the proper tone of voice from a book, obviously, but I do want you to be aware how important it is. Your tone must convey, *without being arrogant or rude*, that you expect to be put through without any delay whatsoever. As sales guru Tom Hopkins says, "Can you put me through please" is *not* a question. Your tone of voice must drop at the end of this statement, exactly the opposite modulation from a normal interrogative. Practice this aloud several times. Say "Can you put me through please," as a statement instead of a question, until it comes naturally.

A related technique is the use of a faux familiarity. For example, if you know the gatekeeper's and the decision-maker's names, you might say, "Hello, Susan? This is Jim Carney. Is Rick in?" I do not recommend this technique, however, as Susan is liable to resent it when she finds out you don't know her from Eve, and every time you score with "Rick" you'll miss with "Rich," "Richard," and "Dick." Nevertheless, I spoke with one sales professional who used this technique constantly. He said he had no trouble reaching decision-makers. "You want to seem like your prospective client's oldest friend. But remember," he advised me, "the second you get through to your prospect, you must be formal and direct. It's not a bad idea to introduce yourself by saying, 'Mr. Prospect, I'll be brief and to the point.' Then you have about twenty seconds to create some interest or start a real conversation."

In either case, always say who you are when you call. This interrupts the gatekeeper's gatekeeping routine, especially if you say your name just a moment after you ask for the decision-maker. For example, "Ms. Jacoby, please. [slight pause] This is Janet Smith calling." If you practice this you will occasionally fluster gatekeepers, causing them to stutter and forget to ask you who you are with and why you are calling.

Another technique to get past gatekeepers is to have a friend place the call for you acting as your secretary. Have your friend reveal as little as possible, creating an ambiguous sense of urgency. It doesn't matter whether this is a local call or long distance. This technique is rich with variables. Here is one scenario, wherein the candidate is a Mr. Fuller:

"Hello, this is a call for Mr. Raymond King."

"Who's calling please?" queries Mr. King's secretary.

"A call is being placed by the office of Mr. Fuller."

"What's this call about?"

"Ma'am, I don't know. I'm just placing the call. Is Mr. King available?"

"He's not available."

"Is there a number where I can reach him, to place this call?"

"He'll be back at four."

"Thank you. We'll try again at 4:15."

You friend need not make any misrepresentation on your behalf. An interesting variation of this conversation is as follows:

"Is this long distance? Are you an operator?"

"No, I am placing this call for Mr. Fuller. He will be on the line shortly."

"And what is the nature of the call?"

"I don't know the nature of the call. I've just been assigned to place the call."

"Well, Mr. King is not available right now."

"I'll inform my calling party."

. . . and so on, never revealing a thing about the caller or the nature of the call. You can leave a message, but you'll get a bigger stir if you never leave a message, never leave a number to call back. By the time you reach Mr. King, he is going to be quite curious as to who this Fuller is, so important he doesn't even place his own calls. In this way you foster and control the urgency of the contact. When calling long distance, a businesslike support-person-to-support-person request such as the following can be terribly successful.

"I have a long-distance call for Mr. King. Will you connect me please. Thank you."

That's it, delivered in one breath, in a detached, matter-of-fact manner.

❋

In the last chapter we discussed how you can use a referral from a more senior executive or even a more senior secretary to get a gatekeeper to put you through to his boss. This creates cognitive dissonance in the gatekeeper. "Will I get in more trouble if I go against the wishes of Mr. Big or if I put this pest through to my boss?" Mr. Big, and his secretary, are usually the winner in this equation—and you get through.

A more disarming technique that many people use with great success is to enlist the gatekeeper in your endeavor. Here again you must know the gatekeeper's name. "Chris, I've been trying to reach your boss for a week now, and I haven't been able to get her attention. Do you have any suggestions for me about how I might be more effective?" When asked sincerely and politely, this usually engenders one of three responses: sometimes it works like magic, a sort of "open sesame," and you will get put through without further ado; sometimes you will get a really useful tip, such as to call at a particular time or put a particular spin on your inquiry, and sometimes you will get told that under no circumstances will you ever succeed in reaching Chris's boss. If you have been unsuccessful for seven days, any of these outcomes is useful.

Remember, before you spend a week trying to reach somebody, verify that you have the right somebody. After about your third message, level with the gatekeeper. "Perhaps you can help me. I'm trying to find out if Ms. Wilson is in charge of advertising and sponsorship sales for the coliseum. Can you verify that?" Don't bark up a tree too long before verifying whether or not there's a squirrel in it. If there is, keep barking.

※

This may seem simple, but if you mail the decision-maker notice that you will call, you can say in all truthfulness, "Yes, he is expecting my call." Sherrill Estes, a professional sales trainer, suggests sending *anything* to alert your targeted contact that you will be calling: "Drop your prospect a card or a note. You don't really have to say what you will be calling about, just that you are going to call. You might write, 'Ms. Durning suggested that you might be interested in a brief meeting with me to discuss your industry. I'd like to have a few minutes to explain her reasoning to you.' It doesn't matter what you write, the point is that when you call you can say, 'he's expecting my call.'"

Of course, in most job-search situations you will have mailed them a query letter such as those you have read in this book, along with your résumé.

※

If you are having trouble reaching your contact, try making a **presumptive appointment** for the telephone call. "Would you please let Ms. Carioca know that I will call her back exactly at 2:00 P.M." It can be highly effective to put similar language in your cover letters. "I will call you on this Thursday at exactly 10:30 A.M. to follow up on this mailing. You can count on me to be prompt. Please advise your secretary to expect my call." Even if she advises her secretary to tell you to forget it, you are further along.

Someone once asked Thomas Edison how he felt about wasting his time trying hundreds of materials for the filament in an incandescent bulb. He responded something like this: "On the contrary. I have not wasted my time at all. I now know hundreds of materials that will not work." Every time you find someone who is truly uninterested in forwarding your job search, you are further down the road to identifying and working with those who will.

Voicemail tends to bollix jobseekers unnecessarily. First of all, every time you make a call, expect the possibility of being routed onto somebody's voicemail. Be prepared to make a great impression, and if you aren't, hang up! George Walther, a professional sales trainer, suggests leaving a message setting a presumptive appointment for a call back (as described above). He also suggests that you have your target paged or ask to speak to her secretary if she is not answering her phone when you call back. So the cure for voicemail is to hit zero or otherwise conjure up a real human so that you can page your contact or speak with her secretary. Try to avoid leaving messages on voicemail more than once or twice a day, even if you call repeatedly trying to reach your party. When you do leave a message, you may wish to be just vague enough to be intriguing: "It was suggested that I call you, and I will be able to put this call through Thursday between three and five in the afternoon, and I would hope that you would be available to chat."

Mr. Walther also has some excellent advice for all jobseekers: "Persistence is the key," he says. "Always do exactly what you say you will when you say you will do it. When you eventually reach your targeted executive, she will already have a strong impression of you as someone who is persistent, who honors commitments, who doggedly pursues his or her objective regardless of setbacks along the way. This is your introduction. Handle this project exactly the same way you will handle major job responsibilities later on."

A major caution about presumptive appointments is that your credibility is entirely shot if you fail to follow through. If you are not someone who can keep a commitment to call back on "Wednesday at exactly 10:00 A.M.," then perhaps you should just say you will call on "Wednesday before noon." Of course if you can't even keep that commitment, you can't run an effective campaign at all.

❁

Whenever possible, cite your referral source. "I was referred to Ms. Cheung by Jason Leong. Can you put me through please." As an interesting point, the gatekeeper doesn't have to have any clue who Jason Leong is for this to work. Ms. Estes says jobseekers should go beyond just citing referrals; they should have referral sources make the initial call. "If you have a referral source," says Ms. Estes, "ask that person for help right when you get the referral. You might say, 'Could you do me a favor—since you know her better than I do—could you just call her up and ask her when would be a good time to visit with her?'"

A personal introduction is always preferable to merely mentioning a mutual acquaintance. Anytime you can get one of your contacts to provide introductions like these, by phone or in person, your credibility is heightened: "Steve, there's someone I know you'd like to meet," or even better, "Steve, I know you could use a strong hand in marketing and there's someone I'd like you to meet." This amounts to an endorsement, a recommendation in advance of your first meeting.

Citing your referral source is also an excellent introduction to a cover letter. "I was discussing remote sensing technologies with Jerome Levinson at M.I.T., and he suggested that you might be interested in someone with my background." With an opening like that, no gatekeeper or screener would keep your letter from its intended recipient.

✷

"Who are you with?" is certainly a troubling question for jobseekers. Its evil twin is, "And what may I tell her this call is regarding?" Many professional secretaries and receptionists have standing orders not to pass through any calls without asking both these questions. *You need to prepare an answer for these before you call,* using one or a mix of the techniques presented here. You can deflect the question by saying something like, "It's about some materials I sent her last week. She is expecting my call," or, "I sent her some materials last week, and I'm calling to follow up." You can also deflect it by citing your referral source: "I was referred to Ms. Durning by Kathleen Dodd. She will recognize that name," or even more forcefully, "Just tell her that Kathleen Dodd suggested that I call." If you are still employed, of course *you are with your current employer,* even if your current employer is in a completely different industry. Some candidates continue their association with their last employer by using such statements as, "This is Bob Johnson, formerly with Hightower Associates." If by any chance you are returning a call, you can preempt "Who are you with?" or "What is the nature of the call?" by saying, "I'm returning her call."

Do not be overly coy in responding to these questions. It is perfectly acceptable to say something like this, "I wrote to Ms. Wellconnected to enlist her help in my job search. She has my résumé, and I am calling to follow up and see if she has any leads, ideas, or referrals to help me in my search. She is expecting my call this afternoon."

As another angle on this whole issue of whom you are with, you can be with your own firm. If you have a particular expertise it can be a great idea to approach employers for contract work and consulting engagements. John Lucht, in *Rights of Passage at $100,000+,* describes in some detail the benefits of this approach for executives and technical managers. If you do some consulting during your job search, you can honestly state that you are "Meridith Lastname, principal of Lastname and Associates." This will intimidate some gatekeepers, as they imagine that you are head of a large and impressive firm. Of course, you should not use this technique unless you are willing to back it up. If "Lastname and Associates" is more a fantasy than a reality, you certainly should not employ such a fiction just to get past gatekeepers.

❄

A tricky method for getting past gatekeepers is to use the implied referral technique. The "implied referral" is simply a language trick: "I was just speaking to Dave Johnson over at Ajax Industrial about something of interest to Mr. Coleman. Is he in?" Then, no matter what happens with Mr. Coleman, you can call the next lead and say, "I was just speaking to Chuck Coleman over at Cog & Wheel about something of interest to Ms. Hardin. Is she in?"

Some people actually look up executives' home phone numbers and call them in the evening. Others call and imply that they are an irate customer, demanding to talk to whoever is in charge of _____, then switch tones completely when they reach their intended party. Sales professionals use these and a thousand other techniques to bypass gatekeepers, but the most effective technique of all is simple persistence. If sales pros will go to such lengths to identify and pitch decision-makers on the phone, won't you take the trouble to pick up the phone and dial it at least once a day for seven days?

❄

PERFORMANCE STANDARD: Try at least seven times to complete any unsolicited telephone contact related to your job search. Call on consecutive days and try to call as early in the day as possible.

What to Say When You Get Through

What do you say when you actually reach your targeted contact? When calling **direct referral sources**, your goal is to have a short but purposeful telephone conversation. In general, try not to ask referral sources out for lunch or a drink—by the rules of etiquette, you will be responsible for the tab. Besides, getting your information by telephone is much more efficient. Ask the questions outlined in the last chapter. You want **ideas**, **leads**, and **referrals.**

Some of your networking contacts will never have met you, so you will need some fairly sophisticated telephone techniques. As mentioned in the last chapter, you want to be able to introduce yourself and ask for what you want in one short little paragraph. For example, if you are a law student or recent J.D., you can compile or obtain lists of fellow alumni who are now attorneys in major firms. You just start at the top of the list and work your way down, getting past the gatekeeper to your targeted contact, introducing yourself, and saying who you are and what you want:

Hello, Ms. Chiang. My name is Antoine Thomás, and I am an alumnus of Vassar and a law student at Yale University Law School. I got your name from Vassar's career office, and I looked you up in the Martindale-Hubbell Law Directory. I will be graduating next spring, and I am interested in joining a firm such as yours. What advice do you have for me, and would you be willing to introduce me to your firm's hiring partner?

Be straightforward, be direct, and remember to push hard for referrals. As long as you stay efficient, do not look down your nose at any referral. You never know which telephone call will strike gold:

"Hello, Mr. Aldus. My name is Alex Simone. I got your name from our rabbi at Temple Beth Emanuel. We were discussing my job search and he mentioned that you work at Astro Tachometer," says the jobseeker.

"Yes, I do, but I don't know how I could help you. I just run the warehouse," counters Mr. Aldus, the networking lead.

"Well, who said I want to meet the president? I wonder if you could tell me who is the M.I.S. manager there?"

"Of course. He just spent six weeks upgrading our whole department. I helped him to understand exactly what it is we do in my department. He was very happy with my help, and said it cut the project time by at least a week. Now I think he owes me a favor . . ."

Although telephone conversations are fine for referral sources, when contacting a **hiring authority**, your goal is to arrange an interview or a brief face-to-face meeting of any kind. I know a candidate who called every major player in her industry and asked each to take just a moment to critique her résumé and see if he had any friends who might be interested in someone with her background. She was nice, insistent, and professional. She had dozens of meetings over this résumé and never changed a word.

Remember, you are approaching hiring authorities about specific types of openings. At this stage in your search, you are not confused about who you are or what you want. You will explore a new opportunity if you come across it, but you are calling with a specific goal in mind. You need to write your own **twenty-second introduction**. Try to weave in some "hot buttons" you think will be particularly enticing to prospective employers: skills, technologies, problems solved, names to drop, even the latest buzzwords in your industry. This is what you will say first when you reach a hiring authority. Here's another example:

Hello, Mr. Jackson. My name is Kelly Barton. I was referred to you by Jan Schade. She said you might be interested in someone with my background. I'm a collec-

tions manager with experience in both public and private hospitals. My strengths include driving a professional collection crew and designing computer-based collection systems to track, manage, and evaluate a range of collection methodologies. I'm calling to see if you have need of someone such as myself, or if you know of anyone who might need a collections manager. I also provide consulting on the design and programming of computer-based collection management systems.

Broken down, here is the skeleton of a typical script for a twenty-second introduction:

Hello, _____. My name is _____. I was referred to you by _____. I'm a _____. My strengths are _____. I'm interested in _____. I'm calling because _____.

Candidates seeking career transitions especially need to be able to present who they are, what they want, and what they have to offer. Here is but one example:

Hello, Mr. Bartel? My name is Eric Slade. I got your name from Eli Perio, and he suggested that I give you a call. I am an attorney with a background in transactional real estate, and I am interested in engineering a transition into some kind of general management position. I have handled recruiting, marketing, and professional development projects for my current firm, and I am a frequent professional speaker, mainly on the topic of all the things that can go wrong with a real estate transaction. My interest is a position in the REO department of a bank or something in corporate real estate. Perhaps a smaller organization would be interested in having someone like myself on board in a dual role as house counsel. At this time I'm mostly trying to get out there and talk to a lot of people, to test the waters. Eli said you know a lot of people I would like to meet.

Before reading further, pull out a pad of paper and draft your own twenty-second introduction as a candidate for a specific type of job. Remember to include both who you are and what you want, and try to convey what is special about you.

❊

There are a few rules of telephone prospecting, which you will ignore to your peril:

1. **Never lead in with a yes/no question, and avoid asking yes/no questions in general.**

2. **Remember to introduce yourself—who you are, why you're calling, and what you want.**

3. Always end your initial introduction with an "easy-out" clause.

You never want the first thing a person says to you to be the word "no." *Never.* In a job-search setting, this means that you want to avoid calling and asking, "Did you get my letter?" This question can be answered four ways: "Yes," "No," "I don't know," or, worst of all, "I'm sure we have, but don't call us. We'll call you." Three out of four possible responses are negative to a jobseeker.

Also, try to avoid asking, "How are you today?" Every two-bit snake oil peddler uses this line. This premature (and usually insincere) query interrupts a good introduction. Any call recipient is going to be uncomfortable with you until he knows who you are and what you want. The sooner and more efficiently you can convey this information, the better.

Finally, even though you may already have spent considerable effort trying to reach this contact, follow the rules of good telephone etiquette. An easy-out clause is exactly what it sounds like; it is an opportunity for the recipient to let you know that you are interrupting a meeting, that her spouse is on the other line threatening divorce, that "60 Minutes" just called and is on its way over with a filming crew, or that she is starving and wants to go to lunch. You will not and cannot have a successful conversation under these conditions anyway. Always end your introductory statement with something like this: "Do you have a second to discuss this, Ms. Highcaliber?"

This brings up the whole issue of sales language, particularly in the first few seconds of conversation. Be positive, affirmative, and confident. Wear a smile on your face and in your voice. Speak without interruption all the way through your introduction.

Try to frame all your job-search queries as open-ended questions, leading questions, or either/or options in which both answers are palatable to you.

1. **Example of an open-ended question:** "What leads or suggestions do you have for me in my job search?"

2. **Example of a leading question:** "Wouldn't your company be interested in turning its security department into a profit center instead of a cost center?"

3. **Example of a question with an either/or option:** "Do you have a moment to get together tomorrow, or would later in the week be better?"

If you learn to frame all your questions in these "can't lose" styles, you will get better answers.

When you reach your decision-maker, talk as though you assume she got your letter but either can't remember what it said or can't remember what she did with it. Just reiterate what was in the letter or go straight into your twenty-second introduction:

"Hello, Ms. Aycharr. I'm glad I finally caught you. This is Sal Ronkin. I sent you a letter and a résumé for the analyst's job. I'm the one with the directly related experience with Urmajor Competitor and the prior background in programming. I wrote a letter describing some of the analytical methodologies I've developed on behalf of Urmajor. Do you have a couple of minutes to discuss the opening?"

In the intro above, note the three components of a good telemarketing intro: does not lead with a yes/no question, quickly establishes who is calling and why, and offers an easy-out clause in the first twenty to thirty seconds.

Your next goal in dealing with a hiring authority is to **ask for an interview.** If you do not have a hiring authority, of course, ask for leads and referrals. Here are some of the questions you will want to pose once you have your contact on the phone.

Questions to pose to potential hiring authorities:

1.   Do you ever have a need for someone like me?
2.   Might you have a need soon? Do you anticipate having an opening in my area?
3.   Would you be interested in discussing contract work? Might you ever need part-time or overflow assistance?

Then, only if you get all negatives to the above do you proceed to these questions:

4.   Who do you know in another department or division who might need me?
5.   Who do you know in another company who might need me?
6.   What ideas, rumors, or grapevine news do you have?

Then, no matter what response you get to any of this, if you are dealing with a decision-maker, *you want an interview.*

I cannot emphasize this enough: If you are talking to someone who *ever* hires someone like you, you want an interview. As we shall see in a moment, it does not matter one iota whether they have an opening, only whether they ever employ anyone like you. In all your contacts with a real hiring authority, your goal is to have a face-to-face interview (unless you are looking for work long distance, in which case you may want an in-depth telephone interview before seeking a face-to-face interview).

Q: What is your goal in any contact with a hiring authority?

A: An interview.

There might be some questions you want answers to while you have your contact on the phone, but your real goal is the interview. If you get an appointment for an interview, *get off the phone!* You cannot sell yourself over the phone. You will have plenty of time to establish rapport and exchange information in a personal interview.

The objective of job-search telemarketing is an interview, and once you schedule that interview you can only damage your candidacy by blabbing on. Get off the phone, call your next decision-maker, and make that next appointment.

✺

Why go to all this trouble? Because you get jobs by talking to people. You talk to people by having interviews. You get to interview ahead of the crowd by calling the employer before she launches a formalized search. You get interviews by cold-calling.

One of my associates told a recent graduate with a degree in mechanical engineering that he should just open up the yellow pages and call companies and firms that he thought might harbor positions of interest to him. This was in Michigan at a time when every major car manufacturer was laying off all levels of staff. My associate told him to simply call and ask for an interview, whether they were hiring or not. "If they say they're not hiring," my associate advised the candidate, "just tell them you want to talk to them anyway, so they'll know what you have to offer in case an opening should come up." This young man went home and did just that—for eight hours a day. Starting without a single lead, he made appointments for eighteen interviews within a week! Experienced engineers were hanging off trees, driving cabs, and learning to macramé at home, yet this candidate landed an engineering job in record time.

Cold-calling works.

✺

Script out your calls. You can start with the scripts you find in this book, rewriting them in your own words. Anticipate the other half of the conversation, develop quick comebacks to the hurdles you know you will face, and, most important of all, *get started.* You will get better with every attempt. Remember the three tenets driving and guiding your search:

- ○ **No technique works 100 percent of the time.**
- ○ **No one application or rejection should define your job search.**
- ○ **Your goal is to improve your odds on *every* application.**

You need to identify hiring authorities, get past gatekeepers, and get appointments for meetings. Make your scripts, then practice, practice, practice. At first, have a friend or a family member play the role of gatekeeper and decision-maker, then start out on companies and contacts that you can afford to bungle, then go on to the key contacts, where you want to use every wile you can muster to get good referrals, job leads, and interview appointments. Above all, *get started.*

As Dale Carnegie suggests, just before you pick up the phone think of the thing that makes you happiest in life. It may be a spouse, a child, a cherished memory from the past. Think of all the things you have to be thankful for. Plant a big smile on your face, grab that phone, and dial. I once knew a salesman who said to himself every time he picked up the phone, "Here comes a hundred dollars!"

For more on cold-calling, read Schiffman's *Cold Calling Techniques (That Really Work!)*, Slutsky's *Streetsmart Teleselling*, and Truitt's *Telesearch*.

Overcoming Objections

Even people with no sales ability whatsoever can get through gatekeepers and reach decision-makers using persistence alone. The bumps in the road start, however, when the decision-maker voices objections.

The novice salesperson may come to a stuttering halt the first time he's confronted with an objection, but an objection is more like a smoke screen than a brick wall. *Any* objection can be overcome. For every objection, there are at least a dozen perfectly good rejoinders.

The goal in dealing with an objection is not to remove it from the speaker's mind, but to keep the conversation going. As an old sales platitude contends, "The sale doesn't even start until the first 'no.'" Objections are more a form of verbal sparring than an attempt to annihilate you and the ideas you are presenting. An objection is not a real obstruction. You cannot accept it at face value. You cannot let it stop your sale.

The most common objections to meeting with you will be:

1. **We're not hiring. We don't need anybody.**

2. **I'm too busy. I don't have time to meet with you.**

When somebody tries to deflect you with "We're not hiring," try one of the following scripts:

1. Whether you're hiring now or not, would you be willing to take a moment to meet with me? If we can establish mutual interest, something is bound to open up sooner or later. Wouldn't you prefer to have a qualified candidate in the wings in case something unexpected develops, rather than having to launch a search from scratch?

2. Even if you don't anticipate an opening, would you be willing to meet with me anyway? I'd like to hear what tips and ideas you have for me, and perhaps you will think of a friend or acquaintance who can use me now. It will only take five minutes. Can we set a time during the day, or would you rather I come after hours?

3. I understand that. I'd still like to meet with you briefly. Even though you don't need anyone now, I'd like you to know what I have to offer. Then if something opens up, you'll think of me first.

4. I'd still like to meet with you briefly. Perhaps you'll think of a friend or acquaintance in the business who could use my services. Maybe you could help both of us out at the same time.

5. I'd still like to meet with you briefly. Perhaps you'll have a lead, referral, or rumor that could be of use to me, and I'd certainly appreciate a moment of your time.

6. Oh, but I'm not asking for a job. I just want a moment of your time, since you know the industry, to see if you have any leads, ideas, or referrals for me. It will only take a moment.

7. I'd still like to meet with you briefly. I've been meeting with several people in this field lately, and perhaps some of what I have learned could be of benefit to you. I'd be happy to share with you what I have discovered, if you would share with me any leads or referrals you may have.

Here are some rebuttals to "I'm too busy":

1. I could help you with that.

2. This'll only take a minute. I'd be happy to meet you anytime you say.

3. I'd be happy to meet with you early, late, or on a weekend if you'd like. I don't intend to interfere with your regular workday.

4. All I want you to do is look at my résumé and think of someone who might be interested in someone with my background. This will only take a moment.

5. Look, I'll meet you after work, I'll buy you a drink, and you just take a look at my background and give me any tips or advice that come to mind. Whaddya say? You name the time.

Remember, you don't actually have to overcome the objection, you just have to keep the conversation going. Stress that you only want a few minutes of your contact's time. Be clear that you will not be a pest or a time hog, and that you will meet with her at her convenience, then go right back into closing an appointment: "Would you be available for such a brief meeting next Tuesday, or would later in the week be better?"

One of the most disarming techniques for an objection is to agree with it. I call this "psycho-judo." For example, in response to, "I'm too busy," you can say, "I understand that, Ms. Jackson. It must be hard to keep track of every detail in a position like yours." Then, STOP, LISTEN, and give your contact a chance to respond.

The usual result is that the conversation just goes on naturally, focusing on your contact's busy life, then gets back to your needs later.

This technique is deceptively effective. Here's another response to "I'm too busy": "Sounds like you need some help down there." Then, STOP, LISTEN, and give your contact a chance to respond. After you listen to your contact's comments, just resume your movement toward an appointment: "Anyway, this will only take a moment. How about Thursday at 2 P.M. sharp?"

✺

If you have not yet mailed in a letter and résumé, here is another common deflection: "Send me your résumé." Jobseekers may hear this a lot, "Send me your résumé and let me take a look at it. Then we'll see about a meeting."

This is almost always a delaying tactic. It is a barrier, an objection, a hurdle thrown up between you and an interview. The bad thing about it is that it often results in another whole round of phone tag.

Recognize this as a delaying tactic and try one of these responses:

1. Let me fax it to you, Joyce, and I'll call you right back.
2. I'd be happy to show you my résumé. Just to speed things up, let me tell you what's on it. . . . Why don't we set an appointment, and I'll bring you a copy in person?
3. What do you need to know, Bob? I'd be happy to tell you right now.
4. I already mailed it to you, but I guess it got lost in the shuffle. Let me tell you what it said. I'm the one who . . .

The other objections you will hear are just as likely to come up in an interview as over the phone, so they are covered in the next chapter.

You will hear this request to fax or send a résumé quite often for the duration of your job search. Résumés are the common currency of the job market. For this reason alone, I am against job-search guides that encourage you to avoid using a résumé. Employers are suspicious of candidates who withhold their résumés. A good résumé is an integral part of a good sales campaign. You should not use one in place of a good sales campaign, but neither should you run a sales campaign without basic sales materials!

There are many variations on job-search strategies. Some emphasize direct-mail campaigns, some say to throw out your résumé entirely and pick up the phone, some say to use a query letter but never provide a résumé, all too many of them focus on pursuing announced openings, which places you smack in the middle of the herd. *All of them will work eventually.* It is readily proven that you can hang a large sign around your neck and walk through the financial district and get job offers, as a fellow named Pete Condon did in Atlanta. Another candidate, an ex-con named Bruce Perlowin, wrote a résumé for sales and marketing jobs with "Ex-Marijuana Kingpin Needs Job" written across the top like a banner. After mailing this to several newspapers, he was inundated with interest. Despite our best efforts, jobseeking can be capricious and unpredictable. You can launch a sophisticated and systematic search and get a job completely out of the blue. Perhaps after months of diligent searching the phone will ring and on the other end of the line is a headhunter who didn't even know you were on the market. Perhaps after working hard to contact employers and sell yourself on your own initiative—as I have outlined in this book—you will end up getting hired by some employer who ran a blind box ad that you responded to months ago.

Nevertheless, no system that does not provide you with a systematic method of identifying, contacting, and meeting with decision-makers is going to be *consistently* effective. In my opinion, the most logical sequence of steps to contacting a hiring authority is the following:

Step 1: Discover the exact name of the hiring authority, usually without speaking directly to that person.

Step 2: Write to the hiring authority by name, enclosing a résumé and specifying that you will call to follow up.

Step 3: Call, penetrate gatekeepers' screens, and ask for an interview, whether the company is hiring or not.

❋

Be prepared to think on your feet and roll with the punches. Your goal is to keep the conversation moving along until you get an appointment. As an example of job-seeker savvy, one candidate I know of returned to San Francisco from a year of teaching English to Japanese business executives. He spent several days exploring the potential for getting a teaching job in the states, only to be told over and over again that he would need a teaching credential, which he didn't have. As he went through the yellow pages looking for private schools that might make an exception, he saw a listing for Polyglot & Babel Foreign Language School. On a whim he decided to call them up and ask them if they needed any teachers.

He managed to reach the director, Dr. Babel, and the conversation was going fairly well when suddenly the director said, "Well, we might be interested in speaking with you. By the way, when you were in Japan did you use the Pearson TOEFL method? We strictly follow the Pearson method here."

"As a matter of fact, Dr. Babel, each teacher was allowed to use his own method-ology. I have always been strongly influenced by the Pearson TOEFL method."

"Great," the director said, "Come on in on Monday and we'll take a look at your résumé."

The candidate then ran out to four or five university bookstores until he found a brand new copy of *The Pearson TOEFL Guide, Instructor's Edition.* He took it home, sat on it, ran over it two or three times with his car, took it to the nearest baseball lot and sifted dust into it, shook it out, and otherwise tried to make it look used as hell. Then he read it cover to cover several times.

On Monday he went to meet the director, with his book under his arm.

"It's amazing how many well-educated people there are looking for work in San Francisco," the director said, patting a fat stack of résumés.

"Tell me about it," said the candidate.

"We have Ph.D.s who apply here all the time. Well, it's really fortunate that you know the Pearson method. Come on, I'll introduce you to the teacher you'll be replac-ing. He's going to Japan, you know . . . ," and down the hall they went.

Direct Mail Techniques to Augment Telemarketing

We have already covered **query letters**, which are letters that you use to contact a person for very broad types of information (see p. 14). Query letters are used to gain informational interviews, either in person or by telephone, to discover more about specific industries, companies, job structures, job titles, and career paths. We also have looked at several examples of **networking letters** (see pp. 40–44). Here is yet another type of networking letter:

Dear Old-Business-Acquaintance:

I am interested in discussing career leads with you. Toward that end I have enclosed a copy of my résumé to update you on my career.

As you can see, I now have 20+ years of officer-level experience in organizations with retail, food, manufacturing, distribution, and sales aspects. I am looking for a challenge, perhaps a young company seeking a period of rapid growth, or a more mature company needing a firm hand at the wheel to engineer some downsizing and cost-containment, either in a particular department, division, or functional area in a larger company, or company-wide for a smaller concern. I will be contacting you within a few days to see if you have any ideas in these areas. Thank you for your consideration.

Sincerely,

A. Smartone

Enclosure.

Broadcast letters are used when you want to contact a hiring authority about a specific type of job. In a broadcast letter, you want to convey that you bring certain skills and experience to the table. Again, it doesn't matter whether the company is hiring or not. The following is a broadcast letter:

Dear Mr. Exactname:

I am interested in discussing career opportunities in the human resources field. Although at this time I am not applying for a particular position, I would appreciate a brief meeting to see if we can establish a mutual interest, and to see if I might fit into your future plans. Perhaps you will find the following worthy of note:

- Extensive background in administrative management, leading professional staff, administering $1,000,000+ budgets, setting/interpreting policy, serving as a bridge between senior management and line managers.

- Solid analytical skills, including budgeting, costing, forecasting, and general statistical analysis. Can design research to resolve management questions.

- Proven recruiter, including providing leadership and training to subordinate recruiters.

- Director of Records and Administration for an organization with over 3000 employees.

I am seeking a position as assistant director of a human resources department or subdepartment, or a specialist/analyst position with opportunity for rapid advancement to the number two slot in a department.

Even if you do not anticipate any staff changes in these areas, I would appreciate the consideration of a brief meeting. Perhaps something will change later, and you will think of me then, or perhaps you have a friend or acquaintance who may be interested in my skills sooner.

Thank you for your consideration. I will be calling you within 48 hours to follow up.

Sincerely,
Your Namehere

Some broadcast letters can be quite clever. If you are trying to create a need for your services, use a **marketing-style cover letter**. When you send a letter like this, you must address it to a senior officer. Your goal is to create a demand for your services, in particular, to replace existing staff that may be performing under par. Every company has deadwood that they put up with, and your goal is to create a desire to replace that underperformer—with you. Here is an example of a marketing-style cover letter:

Dear Ms. Chief-Operating-Officer:

I was referred to you by _____, who said you might be interested in what I have to offer. Most companies spend 50¢ to 70¢ on every sales dollar outside. Are you getting the full value for every dollar spent?

Are your suppliers letting you use their money? Lots of it? Do your suppliers' engineers work for you?

Do your stock orders originate on the factory floor or at the end-user's desk, or does information get handled four times before it is acted on?

Have you applied process control techniques to your human resources, to reward success and weed out failure?

With an engineering background and expertise in MIS, procurement, and materials planning and control, I would like to help you be sure that you are running a state-of-the-art CIM, TQM, JIT, high-technology manufacturing environment. I've enclosed a résumé to give you a quick idea of my background.

Since there are so many ways in which I could assist you in enhancing and maximizing your procurement and materials handling functions, I am proposing that we get together for a brief chat. Surely it's worth discussing.

I will call you on Thursday at exactly 10:00 a.m. Please advise your secretary to expect my call. If you are not available then, have her suggest a time that would be more to your convenience.

I look forward to our conversation.

Sincerely,
I. Gotcha
Enclosure

Specifying exactly when you will call is an effective and new technique. It answers the recipient's rhetorical question, "Now what in hell do I do with *this*?" The answer is, "Hold onto it until Thursday at 10:00 A.M. when this person calls."

Recently, a client who used this technique was forwarded right through to his targeted hiring authority. "You're right on time!" the decision-maker yelled into the phone. This greeting was followed by a long and warm conversation.

One more point about letters to senior company officers: Such letters, especially when accompanied by résumés, are often routed to human resources or other departments. Having your letter routed to the department head you're gunning to replace is pretty useless, wouldn't you say? In the overwhelming majority of cases, having your letter routed to human resources, a passive job creator, is just as useless.

Some of my clients have had success by writing a letter directly to the senior officer's secretary by name. How many letters do you think that secretary gets addressed directly to her? They would enclose a separate letter to the head honcho. In the letter to the secretary, they explained in rather straightforward terms why she should forward the other letter to her boss: "No one else in the company is qualified to evaluate the proposal I am offering," they wrote, going on to request, "Please forward this material to Ms. Bigshot. If she is interested, she will certainly appreciate the consideration, and if she is not, it will only take her a moment to decide that."

Respect secretaries. I have known people who sent flowers and gifts and otherwise tried to bribe or entertain their way past them. Such methods may work sometimes, but you will be much more successful if you can provide a rationale that appeals to their brains. These are responsible businesspeople, and it is far better to have an ally who aligns with you strategically than one who is just humoring you.

Not all of these letters are used to approach employers who want to get rid of deadwood. Sometimes you can win with these letters if the employer is just in the mood for a little reorganization of responsibilities. If you approach an employer during the window of time when he knows he has a problem and before he defines a job and launches a search to solve that problem, you can get that employer to define the job you are seeking *with you in mind*. That is the quintessence of job development.

Another clever idea is to send a potential employer a work sample. Forwarding an insightful analysis of the company's product positioning, or the results of a survey you have conducted, or some other tip or service can be very impressive to a potential employer. Of course, if you reveal that you have nothing to contribute, this will back-fire. For more on this technique, see p. 93 and p. 102.

A **targeted cover letter** is used to apply for a known opening. In this case you fashion your presentation to match a set of known requirements for the opening. Try to include a little personality, and avoid reducing your background to a collection of statistics. Here is one good example:

Dear Ms. Exactname:

With six years of agency experience, I was very interested to see your advertisement for an in-house account executive at Ubuyit Everyday. Your key words, "creative generalist," were particularly relevant to me. When I spoke with my friend Kate Noor, in your department, she said you would be interested in someone with my set of skills.

I have a background of success as an AE, and my success is based directly on my ability to create ad concepts and generate enthusiasm in my accounts. I work daily with full-service agencies, with in-house agencies, and with top brass of client companies. In addition to creative input, I am directly responsible for client budget development, demographics, media plans, and follow through on every detail.

With a Princeton education in psychology and a strong interest in my chosen field, I have maintained a good working knowledge of trends and innovations in advertising, including POS, and some of the most exciting developments in direct response, such as micromarketing and "selectronic" publishing. (Although you may have applicants with more years of experience, I am young and energetic and in the long run, my guess is that my ability to learn and apply new skills rapidly would be of greater interest to Ubuyit Everyday than any specific body of knowledge that I now have.)

I am of course aware of the market position and the public image of Ubuyit as a company, and I would like to stay with a market leader. I look forward to finding out more about the company and its direction for the future.

I trust my background will warrant an interview to discuss this further. My office is not far from yours, and I would be happy to meet with you at your convenience to see if we can establish a mutual interest. I will call you this Friday before noon to answer any preliminary questions you may have, and to arrange a time to meet with you.

Respectfully,

A. Goodone

Enclosure

Incidentally, if they request salary history in advance of an interview, ignore or deflect the issue. Just write "Salary: Negotiable," or "Salary history provided upon interview" at the very bottom of your cover letter, or put a paragraph like this in your letter:

I would be happy to discuss my salary objectives with you in a personal interview. I am sure that if we discover a mutual interest we can come to agreeable terms. Salary is not my first concern, anyway. I am more interested in discussing the position, what challenges you expect the next incumbent to face, and what personal attributes you think would be required for success.

Some employers will exclude you from consideration if you don't comply with requests for salary data, *but far more will if you* do *provide the data.* Salary history or requirements are always exclusionary data. You will never be selected because of your salary history, you can only be deselected.

Never wait more than a day or two at most to follow up on your mailings. More than two days and your letter is gone, tossed into a sorting pile or relegated to some other black hole. You need to predict when your letter will arrive in order to announce when you will call. For this reason I recommend sending your letter by overnight courier or overnight mail (next day), or priority mail (two days between major cities). Within a city, I recommend using messenger services. This doesn't cost very much, and can make a dramatic impact on delivery. (Incidentally, whenever you fax your résumé, follow up with a formal mailing the same day. This protects you in case the fax printing is poor quality *and* gives you two impacts for the price of one.)

Although your letter and résumé should be formal and businesslike, you might consider delivering them in an unusual or unorthodox manner. You might roll them up, tie the roll with a silver ribbon, and place it in a large mailing tube so it has a nice rattle. One candidate I know of sent a box to a film studio. In the box was a plaster cast of his bare foot, his résumé, and a note that began, "My mother bet me I couldn't get my foot in the door . . ."

Another person I know sent in a huge man's shoe. Really huge. This shoe was probably size 18 or bigger. On the bottom he taped his name and telephone number, nothing else. He waited a week and was beginning to wonder if his stunt would work, when the phone rang. "Mr. Bold, we have your shoe. We were wondering what to do with it." He was quick with his response: "Would you like to meet the man who can fill that shoe?"

Some methods I have heard of but would not recommend: One candidate crumpled up his résumé, then wrote on it by hand, "Don't throw this away again. This is the one you want." Another direct mailer, not a jobseeker, wrote on his envelopes: "Open later. Not important." Many candidates have written or stamped "personal and confidential" on their mailings. I even received one once that was perfumed, mailed in a small floral envelope. Some of these techniques garner attention all right, but it is not the right kind of attention. They would be risky enough for entry-level candidates, and I am sure that a management-level candidacy would be greatly diminished by them.

One technique that does work well, however, is to enclose a self-addressed, stamped postcard. This device allows your correspondent to inform you of your status without having to speak to you. When you know you can reach your correspondent by telephone, this would not be ideal, but there will be many times when you can anticipate that you will not be able to phone the decision-maker. Here is one example of this postcard technique:

Dear Your-Own-Name-Here:

☐ Yes, give me a call.   ☐ Call the main number.

☐ My direct line is _____.

OR,

☐ I have forwarded your materials to _____. Please deal with him/her directly.

Remember, use direct mail only to augment your telemarketing campaign. Your goal is to arrange meetings, not have tons of fun licking stamps. "Advertising is what you do when you can't go see somebody. That's all it is," according to Fairfax Cone, the ad man. You have to go see somebody to get a job.

Résumés

Most people have at least a rough idea how to write and design a résumé. Using the methods espoused in this book, résumés do not define your search in the same way they do if you just send in résumés in response to job announcements. If you want to craft a really competitive résumé, use my résumé books. If you are an experienced careerist, use *The Overnight Résumé*. If you are at the entry-level, use *From College to Career: Entry-Level Résumés for Any Major*. Call your local bookstore, or order one from my office in San Francisco, 415-543-2020. For bulk orders, call Ten Speed Press, 510-845-8414.

CHAPTER 6

Sell in the Interview

"You're in the front door, kid. What you do on this side of it is up to you."

—A. J. Carothers, *The Secret of my Success*

Preparing for the Interview

Most candidates blow their first few interviews. Even with diligent preparation, you may go to ten or more interviews before you become a seasoned performer. For this reason, it is a good idea to schedule your first interviews with second-string targets, and to keep interviewing often enough to stay sharp for the duration of your job search. You must prepare for every interview, even if you are going on five or more a week. Every company has a different management style, different challenges, different expectations.

Five Stages of Interview Preparation
1. **Prepare a portfolio of intelligence on the company.**
2. **Prepare a list of skills and technical proficiencies of interest to the employer. Anticipate your potential employer's concerns!**
3. **Compile a list of character traits of interest to the employer. What kind of a person are they seeking?**
4. **Make a list of questions you want to be sure to ask them.**
5. **Make a list of questions you expect to be asked, and practice responding to these queries.**

Research the company in any way you can. Before you meet with a representative from Amalgamated Diversified, see if you can dig up any press articles on the company. Ask the company's public relations or investor relations department for brochures and annual reports. Look in various editions of *Who's Who* and similar references (see Appendix) to see what you can find out about the company's top officers (or maybe even your interviewer). Call the local Better Business Bureau, chamber of commerce, or state consumer affairs board and see if they have any information on the company. Talk to people in your extended network of contacts to see what they know about it. Perform your own market research; call competitors and ask them what advice they would have for someone considering entering this industry, then get around to asking their opinion of Amalgamated. Check for information in any on-line services you can access. Above all, walk into the library and ask for help in researching this company. At least, check the periodicals desk for recent articles in the business and popular press, and check the reference desk for all available listings. You should come away from this process knowing the nature of the company, its position in the market relative to its competitors, long- and short-term economic factors influencing its lines of business, and, if you are savvy, an idea of its reputation and "style."

✳

Next, cruise by your targeted employer's place of business. If you can, find out how people who hold the position you seek dress. *Appearance is critical.* I have seen more than one candidate hired because she had the right look or the right suit. (The rumor is that no one has ever been hired by IBM who failed to wear a blue suit to every interview.) You need a perfect costume. Now is not the time to wish you were ten pounds lighter; now is the time to buy, beg, or borrow exactly the right costume for the interviews you anticipate. *You want to be dressed one step better than your future coworkers' very best everyday outfits.* If you have not done so lately, invest in some new clothes. Pay attention to accessories and details. From your shoelaces to your umbrella, your costume should be complementary and coherent.

If this starts to sound like a calculus of appearance, so be it. I know of one candidate who borrowed a herringbone jacket with leather elbow patches to interview for some kind of writing job in the morning, and switched to his own black suit to apply for a financial job in the afternoon. He was invited back for second interviews by both employers. Had he switched his costumes, he would not have been.

Most people in business can stand by the front door of any company and tell you who is streaming in every morning: "secretary, executive, probably a programmer or computer jock, middle manager, clerk, executive secretary, management wannabe, creative type," and so on.

There are a thousand "looks" for both men and women, and you must get yours exactly right. It is particularly important for older workers to stay current on styles and grooming. If you are out of touch, read the department store advertisements, study people on the street, and visit boutiques and haberdashers to catch up. If you are prematurely grey, consider dyeing your hair or at least touching it up with a little color. A good friend at the barber or salon can shave ten years off your appearance.

One mature candidate I worked with came in with a great track record and a solid network, but his search was going nowhere. I took one look at him and I knew why. In our society, it is rude to say something *to your face* about the shortcomings of your appearance. Everybody will do it behind your back, but no one will do it to your face. This man was paying me to help him in his search, so I was going to give him his money's worth: "You've gained a bit of weight since you bought those slacks. It's fine to be portly, but get rid of that straining belt and buy some braces. Get the kind that button in rather than clamp on; they're never out of style for a gentleman. Second, throw away that plaid tie, the sooner the better. Buy a suit that fits, new shoes, new shirt, haircut, the works. Then let's see how your search goes." It went great.

This man in no way looked ridiculous; he just didn't look energetic and "with it." No matter what shape you're in, you can look stylish. It may cost a bit, but it will cost a great deal more than that to miss out on offers you deserve.

Now that you know more about the company, prepare for your interview by making a list of skills and technical proficiencies that your employer will want you to have. Number and rank them, most important first. Then, scour your background for evidence that you have each skill or proficiency. Here is one example:

Proficiency with Lotus 1-2-3:

○ **Installed Lotus 1-2-3 on new PC LAN, 1990.**

○ **Trained executive secretary on Lotus 1-2-3, 1986.**

○ **Prepared five-year pro formas in Lotus 1-2-3 for proposed building acquisition.**

○ **Because of ability to design visual presentations of data, was selected by president to prepare charts and graphs for first draft of annual report, 1992.**

○ **Attended advanced Lotus 1-2-3 class at extension university, 1992, learning Lotus macro programming.**

Careful interviewees will prepare several pages of such information. There is a hidden benefit to such effort: You will necessarily conduct a mental review of your work history, so you will be more prompt with minutiae from your work past. This beats stammering, "uh, gosh, Jane, to tell you the truth, let's see, I guess I took that training about four years ago . . . I can't remember exactly where we went for that . . ."

Prepare *precise data* to represent these skills and proficiencies. You don't need to memorize it all, but you do need to think of it in advance. Many job-search consultants recommend compiling a master list of twenty or thirty accomplishments that you can use as raw material for this type of preparation.

Next, prepare a similar list of character traits and personal attributes that will be of interest to your next employer. These might include such traits as "stamina," "tenacity," "willingness to travel," or "honesty." Likewise, prepare a list of evidence that you have these traits and attributes. Keep your examples concrete. Claiming that you've "always been thought of as honest and forthright" is vague and begs the question. The fact that you were entrusted to close the shop and prepare nightly bank drops speaks for itself.

Before you go to the interview, make a crib sheet of topics and points that you want to bring up in the interview. Stick a 3×5-inch card in your pocket, or tape a small, unobtrusive note somewhere on the inside of your briefcase.

***

Even savvy jobseekers sometimes fail to get answers to key questions in the interview. They fail to obtain information that is integral to an effective search. Prepare a list of questions that you want to be sure to bring up yourself if they do not come up in the normal course of the interview. In particular, you need to find out how the company's hiring process works and what its plans are for the department you will be working in. You need to know how many interviews will be involved and with whom, what the company's main criteria are for the hiring decision, and what the competition is like. Don't be shy, ask! "How many people are you interviewing for this position?" "What's the competition like?" "How am I stacking up?" "How many interviews do you have planned?" "How soon do you envision someone actually starting in this position?" "When will you be ready to make a decision?" Be sure to ask questions like: "Is there any other information you might want that would help you decide that I am the right person for this job?" To let them know that you view yourself as a strong performer, ask: "If I do a really good job in this position, where can I go in this company?" Finally, find out about your interviewer as a person: "What is your background? What did you do before this? How has *your* career progressed in this company?"

Be careful! Companies feel little or no loyalty to employees these days. Too many of my clients are reporting that they were told they had unlimited prospects with a company, only to be laid off in a few short months when "the company's plans changed." I had one client who was hired by three companies in a row that went bankrupt owing her money! If your sixth sense tells you that the company or the product line is on the ropes, pay attention. A related problem is the boss-from-hell syndrome. Do you want to find yourself working for the boss from hell? Questions to ask are "What happened to the last person who held this job?" "How long did she stay?"

"How does Acme compare to its competitors in this market?" "Is the company currently gaining or losing market share?" "What economic or market trends are affecting the company at this time?" "What are the particular problems and challenges that the next incumbent will face?" "What kind of support—service, engineering, financial, and organizational—will be available to help me perform my job?" "May I have a copy of your annual report?" Here is my favorite method to root out evil: "May I talk to others who currently hold the position I would be taking?"

Make a list of questions like these that you want to pose before you go to any interview.

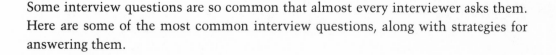

Next, make a list of questions that you expect the employer to ask you. Employers ask questions to get at certain kinds of skills and competencies. They may have a series of questions designed to reveal your computer, technical, and analytical abilities, then a series on communication skills, a series on workstyles, a series on interpersonal skills, and so on. Some throw in questions designed to stump you, to throw you off guard, and to see if you can think on your feet. Right in the middle of the conversation the interviewer may suddenly say, "Sell me this pen."

The structured interview is increasingly popular with corporate hiring managers. The interviewer prepares all the questions in advance, and every candidate hears the same questions in the same order. Some questioners will prepare these questions and then mix them all up, so that one question may be on technology, the next on interpersonal skills, the next on where you grew up, another one on technology, and continuing in random order. Many of these questions may involve reporting past behavior, "Tell me about a time when you . . . ," and modeling future behavior, "What would you do if . . ." Finally, you need to know that some structured interviewers actually score you numerically on answers, reducing your complex skills and personality to a single, final score. Good luck.

Another very common interview style, especially with line managers and less sophisticated interviewers, is a line-by-line review and discussion of your education and experience as presented in your résumé. So, obviously, you should know your résumé by heart.

Given your background, the targeted company, and the particular job you are seeking, prepare a list of questions that you expect your prospective employer to ask.

Some interview questions are so common that almost every interviewer asks them. Here are some of the most common interview questions, along with strategies for answering them.

○ **Tell me about yourself.**

This little command causes more interview hell than any other single phrase. First of all, remember to couch your response in a business context. This is not a request to discuss your home town, your spouse, or your children. The best way to answer this question is to discuss the evolution of your career interests leading to the ultimate, inevitable conclusion that you should work for them. You have already written a twenty-second introduction to yourself. You can use it as a base to prepare a longer presentation with the same conclusion.

○ **What are your strengths?**

Similar questions are "What adjectives describe you?" or "How would you describe yourself?" These are a piece of cake. Describe your strengths relative to the position you are seeking. This is strictly a career and job-related question. Do not tell a lie or overrepresent a skill, but on the other hand, don't fail to mention a skill that is critical for the position you are seeking.

○ **What are your weaknesses?**

This is a bona fide trick question. Your weaknesses must be strengths in disguise. Here is one example: "I have this passion for detail. Sometimes I'll spend too much effort getting something just right. I don't let that stop me from completing assignments on time, but I sometimes do have to work late because of it."

○ **What kind of work environment do you like best?**

There are dozens of ways to ask this same question. "Do you like to work alone or in a team?" "Do you like to work on a computer or with people?" "Can you work with close supervision or do you prefer to work independently?" "Would you rather do bookkeeping or edit letters?" "Tell me about your prior job. What aspects did you enjoy most? Least?" And so on. The correct answer is more or less the true one. Put everything in a positive light, but why lie to get a job sitting behind a computer screen eight hours a day if what you really want to do is deal with people, or vice versa? Be yourself, but sell yourself.

○ **What other types of positions are you applying for?**

This question is designed to flush out your commitment to the career direction you claim to be pursuing. The correct answer is some version of the following: "This is where my talents lie, so I'm applying for other jobs just like this, but with your main competitors." If you are applying for jobs in disparate industries or functional areas, keep that fact to yourself. Nobody wants to hire somebody whose real interests lie elsewhere. I once knew a college professor who was also a bartender. He had two résumés without one single overlapping job.

○ **What do you do with your leisure time?**

This is definitely a trick question. It is designed to discover what sort of person you are and, in particular, to discover if you are someone "like us," us being the interviewer and the rest of the people at the company. Most people in America watch TV in their leisure time, but that has to be one of the worst answers you could give. Be ready to describe leisure activities that would complement the career path you have chosen, or activities that are inherently interesting yet benign. One candidate for an electronics job always made a point of discussing his hobby designing simple toy robots. Avoid controversial items like, "I get arrested in front of abortion clinics nationwide." Saying, "I spend time with my family," might be true, but don't focus on that alone, as some employers fear that family obligations are a direct competitor for the employee's loyalty.

○ **What are your long-term goals?**

Other questions like this are "Where do you see yourself in five years?" and "How does this job fit into your overall plans?" By now you should see a pattern to these answers: The correct answer is five years further along the career path that leads out of this position. It is your job as a candidate to know what that typical career path is. Contrary to what some people think, excessive ambition is not really impressive to employers. One response you can use is to put the question back to your interviewer: "Well, Bob, let me ask you that. Starting with this position, if I were to do a really good job where could I be in five years with this company?"

○ **Describe a problem you had with a former supervisor, and how you dealt with it.**

Some interviewers will try to goad you into saying bad things about former employers. Resist the bait. Answer these questions without slurring your last boss. Some people just refuse to answer by saying: "I've never really had a problem with a former supervisor." I prefer a more subtle response, perhaps something like this: "I had this boss who had a habit of delegating assignments to me and then taking them back before I had a chance to complete them. I sat down with him and told him what he was doing, and that I thought it robbed me of a chance to develop my skills and kept him from getting the effective support I was capable of providing. So he agreed to let me do a major contract proposal if I would get it ready three days early. I did, and he didn't change a word of it. After that he began to rely on me."

✻

Prepare answers to expected questions before you go into any interview, especially any really tough questions you may face, like "Why *were* you in prison, anyway?" and "Why were you fired from this position?" The focus of this book is really too broad to cover every possible problem you may face, but there are some excellent books now on interviewing. My favorites are Medley's *Sweaty Palms*, Beatty's *The Five-Minute Interview*, and Yate's *Knock 'em Dead*. For recent college grads, I like Speck's *Hot Tips, Sneaky Tricks & Last-Ditch Tactics*. You may also be interested in King's *First Five Minutes: The Successful Opening Moves in Business, Sales, & Interviews*, and Walther's *Power Talking: Fifty Ways to Say What You Mean & Get What You Want*. (See Appendix and Bibliography for more information on these and any other books mentioned in the text.

Be careful about "overprogramming" your interview answers. It is not enough just to know a bagful of right answers; you must also sound natural, confident, competent.

You can achieve that only by practicing *out loud*. Conduct mock interviews with your spouse or a friend, tape-record the questions and then run the tape (perhaps while you are driving in your car), or just practice at home, but you must speak out loud to improve modulation and delivery.

Whenever possible, practice with a friend or family member. Have them be tough, doubting your value as a potential hire. Many candidates now use camcorders to videotape their own mock interviews. Seeing yourself on tape can be an invaluable aid to improving delivery. There are interview coaches in major cities, and interview coaching is a part of almost all of the high-end outplacement programs, but the benefit is in the doing—whether you do it in the kitchen at home or in a consultant's office on the thirty-third floor of a highrise.

Here are some questions to practice on:

○ What are your salary requirements? What is your salary history? How much do you make where you are now?

○ If you won the lottery, what would you do in the first six months?

○ Have you ever been fired?

○ Tell me about yourself.

○ What are the major responsibilities in your current job?

○ Sometimes people get a little excited around here. How would you handle it if somebody yelled at you?

○ What are your values? What is important to you?

○ We've never had a (woman/male/minority/Ph.D./you name it) on the staff here. Do you think this will pose any problems for you? How do you propose to handle that?

○ Tell me about a major failure in your life and how you dealt with it.

○ What job did you like most? Why? What job did you like least? Why?

○ What job functions have you found most difficult to perform?

○ What is your greatest accomplishment, and how did you achieve it?

○ How would you improve yourself?

○ If you were your own boss, what things would you do differently in your present company/department?

○ What are your strengths?

○ Where do you see yourself in five years? Ten years? What are your ambitions?

○ What can you tell me about your family?

○ Some of our clients are in Europe. Do you know what time it is in Frankfurt?

○ What's the best job you've ever had? Why?

○ What kind of grades did you get in college?

○ If you were to join us, what risk might we be taking in hiring you?

○ What is the meaning of life?

○ How did you pick your career?

○ What motivated you to make the career transitions I see in your background?

○ To whom did you report in your last position?

○ How do you motivate subordinates? What is your supervisory style?

○ Who was the best boss you ever had? Why?

○ How many hours a week do you usually work? Do you take work home or do you try to get it all done at the office?

○ What does success mean to you?

○ How do you account for this gap in employment on your résumé?

○ So, what do you think of our little operation?

○ What do you know about our company?

○ Read any good books lately?

○ What are your weaknesses?

○ Why have you had so many jobs?

○ This job seems a little out of your normal realm, wouldn't you say?

○ We have a lot of Pacific Rim suppliers. Do you know what time it is in Taiwan?

○ Have you been looking for a job for very long?

○ What kind of work environment do you like best?

○ What are some of the reasons you left this job? How about that one? That one?

○ What are your boss's strengths? Weaknesses?

○ Why are you trying to make this transition?

○ What did you tell your current employer to get time off today?

○ What type of people do you like to work with most? Least? Have you ever worked in an office with bad politics? Tell me about that.

○ What do you do with your leisure time?

○ Are you more of a lone eagle or a team player? Pick one and tell me why.

○ What kinds of customers have you been dealing with?

○ What is your salary history?

○ When you say you know this computer program, what does that mean? Give me an example.

○ What are some of the drawbacks to the job you have now?

○ What organizational contributions can you tell us about? Did you contribute any operating procedures? Report formats? Information flows? Strategic approaches?

○ How do you deal with change?

○ What are your salary requirements?

○ When would you be available to start?

○ Which of these accomplishments on your résumé are solo efforts and which are team efforts?

○ How did you hear about this opening? Do you know anyone who works at this company? What did they tell you?

○ Describe your current boss. What is her management style?

○ How did you get your last job?

○ Where do you see this industry heading?

○ What other jobs are you applying for?

○ What do you mean by "mutual decision"?

○ Given our objectives as I've just explained them to you, how would you organize this department?

○ What do *you* want to get out of this job?

○ If you were hired for this position, how would you organize your day? How would you prioritize your tasks?

○ Why are you applying to us? Why do you want to work here?

○ What do you do in your leisure time? What do you do outside of your job that interests you?

○ How would you describe yourself? How would your friends describe you? How would your current/former employer describe you?

○ What is your greatest accomplishment? How did you do it? Why do you consider this your greatest accomplishment?

○ Describe a team project you were in charge of. How did you delegate assignments? How did you monitor each team member's progress? Describe the decision-making process within the team.

○ What were the major challenges in your last position? How did you plan and execute your response to these challenges? How successful were you in dealing with them?

○ What would your closest coworkers say about you in confidence to someone else?

○ If you had to go on a trip to Mars, what five things would you take with you? What five people?

○ Describe the employee review process at that company. How did you review your subordinates and what were the criteria? Of those criteria, which did you think were actually the most important?

○ How were you yourself reviewed? What kind of ratings did you receive? Concerning your own position, which criteria did you view as most important? How did you rank on those criteria?

○ You have two drinking glasses, each the same size and each half full of liquid. You pour one into the other, but the second glass is still not full. What happened? Give me as many scenarios as you can.

○ What's the most disappointing project you ever worked on? How could you have turned this around?

○ Why should I hire you?

○ If you were in charge of this department, how would you manage resources? How would you motivate staff?

○ Tell me what's good about this paper clip. Now tell me what's bad about it.

○ Describe a case in which you made a suggestion to senior management. Did they implement your suggestion? If not, why do you think they chose to ignore your recommendation?

○ Tell me a story.

○ Considering your workstyle, what characteristics and approach would the best boss for you have?

○ Are you detail-oriented or do you like to focus on the big picture?

○ Sell me this pen.

○ What do you do on your vacations?

○ What is your computer background?

○ If you could live anywhere in the U.S., where would you choose to live?

○ How much travel would be acceptable to you? Do you like to travel? Do you have any restrictions on your availability for business travel?

○ Do you smoke?

○ What kind of performance do you think you would be expected to deliver in this position we've been talking about?

○ What is your attendance record like? Do you mind if I call and verify that?

○ Have you ever trained or supervised subordinates? Can you describe that?

○ What are your hobbies?

○ Have you ever represented your company to the press? How did it go?

○ What capabilities would you like to develop in yourself?

○ What motivates you? What kinds of things are important to you?

○ What are your limitations?

○ What would your references say about you?

○ Would you discuss your approach to dealing with stress?

○ Tell me your life story, but keep it short.

○ What are your personal objectives in seeking this position?

○ What kinds of skills do you like to use most? What are "favorite tasks" for you?

○ It takes stamina to succeed in this position. What in your background would indicate that you have this type of stamina?

○ How would you handle an irate customer?

○ Describe your writing skills, and use examples of specific projects to illustrate your abilities.

○ Nobody's perfect. What does "perfect enough" mean to you?

○ Where did you grow up?

○ Are you a better listener or presenter?

○ I'm kind of a nut about background checking. Let's just say I'm good at it. Is there anything you would rather tell me now, rather than have me find out about it later?

○ Do you have any questions?

Interview Protocol

At the management level, try to schedule no more than two interviews per day, one as early as possible in the morning, and one anytime after lunch. Always call the afternoon before your appointments to confirm that you will be there as scheduled. Be sure to arrive exactly five minutes early. Being late to a job interview is universally considered *a very bad sign.* Many employers consider it *the kiss of death.* No excuse will be acceptable. Even being one minute late is too late.

Several years ago I had a client who failed to confirm a meeting. The human resources representative had tried to call him to confirm because she had convened a panel of managers for the interview and wanted to be sure everything went smoothly. His tape machine had the flu so he never got the message. He arrived at the appointed place and time, but the meeting went poorly. The daily schedule of every manager on the panel had been in limbo until the very moment that candidate walked in the door. They took out their frustration on him, and every aspect of his background and qualifications was scrutinized severely. Even though he had sterling credentials, they hired someone else.

Always call to confirm. Always show up exactly five minutes early.

Your interview kit should contain a few extra résumés, copies of any correspond-ence you have already had with the company, interview crib sheets, a pad of paper, and at least two functioning pens. Don't forget personal grooming supplies.

Allow plenty of time for transportation, getting lost, fixing your hair, and similar emergencies. I know of one candidate who drove to a meeting only to look down and see athletic shoes on her feet. She had meant to change to dress shoes, but had forgot-ten. She searched the car, finding not another pair of shoes. So she raced to the nearest mall, made the manager of a shoe store open early, bought a pair of shoes, and made it to her interview just in the nick of time. Plan to arrive early enough to wait a few minutes outside the office, then walk in exactly five minutes early.

If for any reason you are detained by another appointment, call and postpone your interview. This is professional protocol. Do not call and ask to come in "a few min-utes late." Call, let them know you have been unavoidably detained at another appointment (don't go into details), and ask to reschedule the appointment at their convenience.

Once you step into the office, your interview has already begun. Be exceptionally cordial with the gatekeeper. Be patient and at ease as you wait your turn. That gate-keeper is the decision-maker's eyes and ears. Anything you say can and will be used against you.

You may have to wait quite some time. Go over your notes or otherwise look pro-ductive. Don't veg out with a pop novel or waiting room magazines. How long should you wait? You are here to convey that you are a valuable person. If you are a valuable person, then your time is valuable. Wait only as long as someone of your stature would wait for a medical appointment. Then, if you have not gained entrance to the inner sanctum, rise and inform the receptionist, "I'm so sorry. I have other appoint-ments today. Would you please let Mr. Big know that I may need to reschedule this appointment. Could you find out if he is ready now, or if not, what other times he may have available?" Let not a hint of anger enter your voice. Business is business.

When you finally step into the meeting, look your interviewer in the eye, greet her, commit her name to memory, and shake hands firmly but smoothly (a handshake should never be a demonstration of strength). Take a seat only when one is offered. Sit up straight, and lean slightly forward in your chair. Remember to smile naturally and often. You are on stage. The curtain is up and the lights are on. Now is the time to be yourself, but sell yourself.

In the first few *seconds* of your meeting, the interviewer will already have formed an opinion of you. That is why your appearance and initial demeanor are so darned important.

There are many different types of interviewer. Some ramble, allow a lot of interrup-tions, and forget your name. Some use a structured series of questions and will not deviate from them no matter what. Some are aggressive, even intimidating. Most of them just want to find out what your skills are and what kind of person you are.

What the employer wants to know:

○ **Can you do the job?**

○ **Would they like to work with you?**

Empower yourself as an interviewee; don't be a passive player. The most savvy jobseekers turn the interview around and interview the interviewer. In the first few minutes you want to wrest control of the interview long enough to get answers to a few preliminary questions of your own. It is particularly important that you find out what kind of candidate the employer is seeking before you go off in the wrong direction. Once you know what the hiring authority's criteria are, you can slant all your answers to demonstrate that you meet or exceed these criteria.

Most interviews start out with a few pleasantries and then the interviewer signals the beginning of the interview with "Tell me about yourself" or "What interests you in our company?" or a similar line. Don't rush the pleasantries. Your goal is to find something in common. Find a connection, no matter how tenuous. "You're from Sasquatch! That's not too far from where I grew up." "What a coincidence. I used to work for them, too!" "Smartleton! That's your alma mater? My niece is going to school there now."

Whenever possible, try to take control of the interview for a few moments just before the structured questioning begins. Ask questions like this:

Where do you see the product line going? What talent will you need to achieve your immediate goals? What skills and abilities are you looking for in a candidate for this particular type of position we are discussing today?

Or, if the interviewer has already begun structured interviewing, try to break in gracefully:

Before we go into that, could you take a few seconds to tell me about the company and the position that is open?

You want answers to questions like the following. Of course, as specified earlier, you will have prepared these questions in advance:

Questions related to selection criteria:

○ What challenges face the next incumbent?

○ Where does the company see this department/product line/function going?

○ What particular knowledge or skill would be most critical for success in this position?

○ What personal attributes, as opposed to any particular knowledge or skill, do you feel are most critical for success in this position?

Questions related to management style:

○ What do you expect of the next incumbent?

○ How will that person's performance be evaluated?

○ How will all parties work together?

○ What are the opportunities for advancement?

After you have a handle on the company, the position, and the selection criteria, then you can either hand the power back to the interviewer and be interviewed, or you can make a presentation of your background relative to their requirements.

CAUTION: With some people, particularly professional interviewers, you will not be able to wrest control from them for one moment. If you try and are thwarted, you have lost nothing. Just go along with the interview like everyone else.

※

When there is no known opening and you have arranged an interview either to obtain leads or to present your candidacy for a future opening, then you will naturally control most of the interview. Find out about the company, how the jobs that you are interested in are structured in that company, how the company conducts its hiring processes, and when your contact anticipates that they might actually need someone like yourself. *Always find out who originates job orders.* It is not always obvious. Find out who decides that the company needs to design a new job or launch a search to fill an opening or an expected opening.

Then, make a full presentation of who you are and what you have to offer relative to their future needs. This can take as few as ten minutes, but don't rush the meeting if it is friendly and you are getting good information. Most of all, you want the name of the hiring authority and permission to contact him on a regular basis. Try to get fax numbers and direct dial telephone numbers everywhere you go in life.

You can also show work samples to pique the interest of reticent or we're-not-hiring employers. I know an artist who wanted a job in art, any job in art. She showed her drawings of angels to a company that carved tombstones, and got a job as a designer. Another candidate wanted a newspaper job, but had no college degree and no experience whatsoever. She estimated that her chances for winning a competitive placement were virtually nil. But she had gumption. She covered a city council meeting in an up-and-coming suburb and sent it to the state's largest newspaper. She was hired as a stringer.

This is new job creation, and it is the epitome of good job searching.

❋

There are a few rules of interviewing etiquette that you will ignore to your peril:

○ Make eye contact, but don't stare down your interviewer.

○ Never contradict, interrupt, or argue with your interviewer. This is interview suicide.

○ Be alert, act interested, focus on the positive.

○ Never, never, never say anything bad about your former employers.

If you have to bite your tongue and speak in codes only you yourself understand, never say anything critical about former employers. "I can't say enough nice things about them" can certainly be taken two ways. Rightly or wrongly, hiring officers usually think someone else's bitter, disgruntled employees are the worst hires in the world.

Don't be afraid to say "I don't know," "Let me think about that. Can we come back to this in a minute?" and "I'll find out and get back to you."

Please, do the world a favor and don't contradict, interrupt, or argue with your interviewer. To paraphrase Dale Carnegie, "Nobody ever wins an argument." You don't have to parrot every political and business opinion he mouths, but in general it is a good idea to keep your disagreement to yourself. If asked for your business opinion, give it honestly, but if you disagree with your interviewer, couch your response in respectful language. "I can see how you would think that aviation widgets simply can't lose in this marketplace, and you may very well be right, but I think space widgets stand a chance to gain market share." Soften your differences with qualifying phrases: "I understand how you could . . . ," "I could be wrong, but . . . ," "It could be that . . . ," "I believe . . . ," "I think that . . . ," and words like "perhaps" and "maybe." A know-it-all is not usually considered an attractive hire.

Try to answer the question that was asked. If you don't understand it, have it clarified. Say "I'm not sure I understand your question. Can you rephrase that?" or restate the question yourself, "I'm sorry, I'm not sure I understand your question. Do you mean _____?" Be careful and exact. Any failure in communication will be considered your fault! Candidates who go off on tangents or fail to answer the questions as asked are considered dim bulbs. Try to get feedback from the interviewer on how you are coming across: "Does that answer your question?" "Would this kind of experience be useful in the position you are recruiting for?"

Anytime you get flustered in an interview, ask a question. The question will give you an element of control. Whoever is asking the questions is in control. For example, if the interviewer just stops and stares at you, an old-fashioned stress interview technique, just pause and then say, "Is something wrong?"

Avoid discussions of salary and perks until late in the hiring process. If you seem more interested in the perks than the job, you will be out of contention. On the other hand, if you agree to a low-ball range before the employer is committed to you, it is very hard to build that range back up later. If salary comes up prematurely, ask your contact what salary they had in mind for the position. Then use lines like these: "We're in the same ballpark, but I am really more interested in the job and what it entails. Can we come back to this later?" Or, "That seems a little low for what you are expecting from this position, but let's talk further because I really like the company and the people I've met so far." You have no leverage over salary negotiations until the company has a definite interest in hiring you. If you must name a range, name a large one. "Well, I have been making in the high 40s, plus a liberal package of bonus, allowance, and overrides amounting to considerably more. Anyway, as long as you are paying a competitive salary, I am sure we can come to terms. What I want to know more about is . . ."

Finally, when in an interview for a known opening, there is one more rule and it is a critical one: **If you want the job, you must state your interest unequivocally**.

No matter how interested you are, and how animated you seem about the opportunity under discussion, you absolutely must state that you want the job. Hiring officers will not assume interest on your part short of an explicit statement. Although you may not want to be so blunt as to say, "I want this job," be sure to say something as clear as this: "The job as you have described it to me sounds perfect, Mr. Warren. I am very interested in this opportunity. How do we proceed from here?"

As discussed earlier, always find out what happens next. You want to know how many interviews to expect, when the decision will be made and by whom, what the competition is like, and other information on the hiring process itself that will help you to excel as a candidate. Ask these questions:

○ How many people have you seen?

○ How many people do you have left to see?

○ Of the people whom you have seen, where do I stand?

Then, if you're not number one:

○ What's the difference between me and the person who is at the top of your list?

If you want to close a job offer, use closing language. Ask something like this: "Given what you know about me now, Ms. Johnson, is there any reason we couldn't work together?" Or you might say, "Ms. Johnson, this job sounds perfect. What would I need to do to convince you to offer me this position?"

Then, when you encounter objections, overcome them. For example, "overqualified" is a code word for "too expensive" and/or "too old." You can stress that your experience would be a great benefit as they face the projects and challenges coming up, and let them know that you are in a financial position where you can now take a job that pays a little less, as long as it meets your need to be challenged and contribute to a greater good.

Incidentally, if you are going for an entry-level job or the company is desperate to make a quick placement, you will want to be one of the first candidates interviewed.

It is common for a company to shut down new interviews when they have enough viable candidates. They may also offer the job to one of the first candidates interviewed, and she may accept. Then the search is over.

On the other hand, in a typical management-level search, it is better to be one of the last people interviewed. Your competitors will have made their presentations, and you can discover your relative position and strength. You are in a much better position to overcome objections to your candidacy and force the employer to make a decision (either to hire you or include you in continuing rounds of interviews). If you are one of the first or second interviewed, you won't know where you stand and the employer will necessarily be noncommittal no matter how strong your qualifications may be. These are compelling reasons to try to be one of the last candidates interviewed. Ask when interviews start and when the employer hopes to end the first interview cycle, then have "scheduling difficulties" until you get the slot you want.

Finally, as far as interview protocol and etiquette goes, if you discover you do not want the job, tell the recruiter at the earliest possible moment that you are not a candidate. Even if the job or the company is absurdly wrong for you, be graceful. If you find you are not interested in a position, be forthcoming with that fact. "This job doesn't seem exactly right for me, Ms. Collins. I really had in mind more of a customer service or public relations function than a direct outside sales position. I feel that my strengths are teamwork and collaboration, and it sounds to me like what you need is more of a lone-eagle type. I appreciate the opportunity to meet with you and learn about Amalgamated Diversified, however. You know, I have a friend I think would be perfect for this position. Let me give you her name and number, and I'll call her and let her know about the opening, as well."

✸

Don't leave a meeting without coming to one of two conclusions. Either you want the job and think you have a chance at it, or you don't.

Two possible outcomes to a meeting:

1. There is interest (yours or mutual) and you try to set an appointment for the next interview and discover the names of the other persons you need to meet before the final decision can be made.

2. You are satisfied in your mind that there is no potential placement at this time, and you extract leads, referrals, and lines of communication for follow-up networking.

Never leave a meeting without finding out what happens next. "When can we meet again, Mr. Bartoli? I'm ready anytime you are." If there is interest, force your way into a second interview appointment before you leave the first one, and a third before you leave the second, and so on. You should note that companies are requiring more and more interviews now. Some placements take five, six, or even more interviews before a decision is made.

If they give you a "don't call us, we'll call you" line, follow up with this one: "I know you'll be getting back to me. At what point—if I don't hear from you—should I be back in touch with you?"

If an interview doesn't lead to candidacy for an opening, get leads and referrals instead. Try particularly hard to get a referral to someone else in the same company you are interviewing with. If you bomb at headquarters, ask to meet with a branch or division manager. This is a strong referral when you go to meet with that person; to him, you will have been "sent out by headquarters." Collect business cards from everyone you contact in your search. Every contact you can call again is a contact that can lead to your perfect job. *Check back in with all your referral sources once every two weeks,* at least. A quick call to see if they have any new leads, rumors, or referrals is sufficient.

This process of checking back can be highly productive. Employers who initially reject or deflect you can be very receptive to your candidacy when something does open up. If you check in with them on a regular basis, they will feel as if they already know you.

WARNING: Do *not* press for leads when you are a contender for a known opening. This is an indicator that you either lack confidence in your candidacy or don't actually want the position.

Interview Follow-up

After every interview, you should immediately summarize the meeting on your 5 × 8-inch lead card. Pay particular attention to recording the employer's key concerns. Try to infer his motivating factors. For example, his last assistant may have been great at spreadsheets and reports, but she was lousy on the phone and a sloppy dresser. Even if spreadsheets comprise 90 percent of the job, the "hot buttons" for this hiring authority may be customer service skills and personal appearance. This human factor must be taken into account in your efforts to cinch this job.

A full-scale job search will involve hundreds of contacts, and in no time at all you will need these notes to refresh your memory.

Of course, you should record the date of next contact, such as "Get references to Dave by Friday" or, "Decision to be made by next Wednesday. Call Dave Wednesday after lunch if he hasn't called me first."

Next, write that thank-you note or letter and get it in the mail! See the next chapter for more information on thank-you notes and post-interview lobbying to win a position.

CHAPTER 7

Close the Deal

"Employers don't like to hire strangers."
—J. Michael Farr, *The Very Quick Job Search*

Keeping Your Candidacy Alive Through Multiple Interviews

Recently one of my clients was offered a position in a first interview and it nearly scared him half to death. The recruiter had failed to hire enough candidates to fill a management training class, and I think if the janitor had come to work early he'd now be an insurance underwriter. My client decided that he couldn't take a risk on this type of offer. What is the value of a commitment offered so freely? Would you marry someone who proposed to you on the first date?

Very few people are hired in a first interview these days. You can expect multiple interviews, delays, investigations, and intrigue. This post-interview period has become so critical that a whole book has been written about it, *The Perfect Follow-Up Method to Get the Job*, by Jeffrey Allen. Another excellent source on this topic is chapter 11 of Tom Jackson's *Guerrilla Tactics in the New Job Market*.

To turn mutual interest into a job offer, you have to manage a steady stream of correspondence and telephone contacts with the decision-maker.

Seven Ways to Influence the Employer After the First Meeting

1. Write a thank-you letter promptly after every interview.
2. Telephone with a new thought or comment related to the interview.
3. Perform a task (the Herculean approach).
4. Send a substantive follow-up letter.
5. Send a human interest follow-up letter.
6. Send a continuing interest letter.
7. Have a reference call or write to promote you.

After every meeting, go home and write a thank-you letter or note and get it in the mail that same evening. It is more important that a thank-you letter be prompt than that it contain any particular information. Here is a simple example:

Dear Ms. Orr:

Thank you for your time today. I was impressed by Orr Industries, and
I hope a tax analyst position opens up before summer. I'll be calling you
once every couple of weeks, as you suggested. Also, thanks so much for
the referral to Jason T. Colson. We have an appointment already.
Again, thank you, and I'll be in touch.

Sincerely,
Your Name Here

For many candidates, it is acceptable to type such letters onto formal thank-you
notes available from any better stationer. Do not handwrite anything except the
briefest of notes. Handwriting denotes intimacy, and is not appropriate in a job
search. If you are an executive, or if a thank-you note is just too informal for your
style, then type the thank-you letter onto monarch-sized stationery ($7\frac{1}{4} \times 10\frac{1}{2}$-inch).
Try to avoid typing short letters on full-size stationery. If you meet with several
people, send each and every one of them a follow-up note. If you meet with someone seven times, you should send him such a follow-up note seven times.

Believe me, many management hiring decisions come down to etiquette. All the
finalists will be technically qualified. The only way to separate the losers from the
winner is through evaluating each candidate's image, presentation, enthusiasm for the
opportunity, and follow-through on details.

A warm and genuine letter of appreciation is always best, but even a perfunctory
letter is fine. Again, the important thing is prompt, graceful follow-through; content is
secondary.

❊

The thank-you letter is also an excellent place to recover from a gaffe in the interview
or to overcome objections raised by the employer. Never let an employer voice a per-
ceived shortcoming in your candidacy without addressing it. Here is an example:

Dear Kathleen:

I am writing to thank you for taking the time today to meet with me to dis-
cuss your combined staff development/internal consultant position.
Enclosed is a list of prior employers you may contact for references.
Please do not contact my current firm until we have explored this further.

Kathleen, you mentioned that several of the candidates you had under consideration had more formal training experience, and that comment has been on my mind all evening. Although we discussed my recent positions in some detail, they are all positions in which I handle a wider range of functions than just training and development. You should know that for five years I planned, facilitated, and delivered sales training and motivational programs for Smokenders, Inc., and for three additional years I was a full-time presenter for a worldwide tour operator. With Smokenders we used the kind of quantitative training/measurement system you want someone to implement for you.

I also forgot to tell you that my associates in the Legal Administrators Guild selected me to deliver two seminars at last year's annual conference in Dallas: "Human Resources Update: New Laws, New Decisions," and "Teaching Rainmaking to New Associates." You can rest assured that my curriculum design, testing, and platform skills are more than sufficient to achieve your staff development goals.

Although you may be inundated with résumés from training specialists, I feel that I have a great deal more to give because of the breadth of my background. We discussed my organizational development accomplishments and you seemed quite impressed with them. Perhaps you could share some of the details with Rob, who mentioned that this was his number one criterion for this hire. In short, I can offer the company a management mentality, an understanding of overarching goals and objectives, and a proven ability to turn around difficult office cultures and make them performance-oriented and successful. I think we have a pretty good match here.

I will call on Friday before noon to answer any follow-up questions you may have. I appreciate your interest.

Sincerely,
D. Jobhunter

Of course, if you write a long letter, it should be on full-size, 8½ × 11-inch paper.

You can also telephone in such a new spin on your interview, although you *must* still write a thank-you note. Simply call the decision-maker and deliver the kind of rationale demonstrated in the letter above, either providing new data or a new spin on the existing data. "Bob, I was thinking about our meeting last night and I realized there's a couple of things I forgot to tell you . . ." If you suspect it will take you three days of phone tag to reach your decision-maker, you'd probably be better off putting the information in a letter and calling back to let them know you would be happy to answer any questions about it.

The follow-up call can be very effective when combined with the strategy of performing a task for the potential employer. Employers are impressed when candidates actually do something for them prior to the hiring decision. Show some initiative and enthusiasm for the tasks required in your targeted position *before* you even have a job offer. In the last chapter you read about the artist drawing angels and the writer sending in an unsolicited news piece. Here are two more examples:

Marsha Kudzu was a candidate for a management position with a small business. The owner liked her and thought she could do the job, but he wasn't sure he could afford the salary she demanded. She designed and conducted a survey and analysis of his competition and gave it to him. He hired her.

Paula Schiffn was a candidate for a senior sales analyst position. The V.P. of sales mentioned in the interview that he wanted to database customer account information using a certain program. She called him back the next day to let him know that she had looked into that program and it was not powerful enough to meet his needs. She suggested another program. He suggested she put it in for him.

Think of some task or service you can provide to a potential employer to demonstrate your interest, commitment, and relevant job skills. Find something out, look something up, check something out.

At any time after your interview you can write follow-up letters commenting on some item that came up in the interview. This can either be substantive, for example, forwarding information you come across relating to the employer's product lines or markets, or it can be a human interest piece, such as an article about his home town or his favorite sport. Every three to five days, your targeted employer should receive something in the mail with your name on it. If you need to, send in a new reference once in a while, anything to keep your name before the decision-maker until the hiring process is complete. Scour the business, trade, and popular press for articles you think might be of interest to your hiring authority. Cut them out, clip a note to them, and send them in. "Thought you might be interested in this. —Jon von Darman." Search particularly for news on the company, its competitors, or economic and market trends impacting its lines of business.

Of course, all during this process you are pursuing continuing interviews. Don't worry if you are not the company's first choice, as long as you are in the running. Perhaps the first-choice candidate will accept another position before the company can make a decision, the number two choice will decide she doesn't want the offer, and the third choice will have a bad reference that isn't discovered until late in the process, the number four choice will fail to show up for one of his interviews, and the number five choice is you. It's not over until it's over, and as long as you are in the game, play your hardest.

If you are unable to reach your contact by telephone, or if you originally applied to a blind box ad, you can send a continuing interest letter. This is a letter that simply states that you are still interested in the opportunity and would be happy to pursue the matter if they have any interest. Here is an example:

Dear B. A. Stonewall:

This letter follows up my application for the position of environmental engineer (Staff Engineer II).

Please know that I remain quite interested in this opportunity and am eager to discuss the position. I feel a one-on-one meeting will answer any questions you have about me.

As stated in my résumé, I am experienced in a wide array of industrial hygiene responsibilities, from testing to process analysis to employee training. I feel that with my technical skills as developed as they are, I am prepared to step in and make an immediate contribution.

I thank you for your attention on my behalf, and I look forward to your call.

Sincerely,
B. A. Phoenix

A truly effective technique is to have one of your references call and recommend you: "I heard you were considering hiring Alice Tobías as an account rep. She mentioned that you might call. Since I'm out of the office a lot, I thought I'd just ring you. Listen, if you can bring her on board you'll have a gold mine on your hands. Most productive employee I've ever had . . ." Of course, as mentioned earlier, it's even better if you can have one of your references introduce you to a potential employer in the first place.

Creating Momentum

As your interviews progress, continue asking questions about the company and the hiring process. Be sure to ask, "How soon will you be ready to make a commitment?" Stress that you can be ready to make a decision as soon as they are ready to make an offer. The search process is a ritual, and you can force it to a premature conclusion by performing each obligation on your part at the earliest possible moment. If they ask for references, fax them in within twenty-four hours. If they ask for another interview, press for one of the earliest possible appointments. (After the players have been named, being last to interview is no longer critical. You want to be the first one to receive an offer, not the last one to be fully evaluated.) In this way you can create momentum in the hiring decision. Once you have jumped through every hoop, dotted every "i," crossed every "t," and told them you're ready to respond to an offer, they will feel obligated to give you a decision. If you are lucky, prompt, and enthusiastic, you get an offer while your competition gets a "Sorry, we've already made a decision."

On the other hand, if a company stalls you, take it gracefully and don't give up. Just keep sending them some kind of positive message every three to five days. Unless they tell you that they have made an offer to someone else and that person has accepted that offer, you still have a chance. Most companies will not tell you when they extend an offer to someone else; they will just stall you while they wait to see the outcome of negotiations with the other candidate. You cannot always tell why a company is stalling, so keep up your effort until you get an offer or they tell you that someone else has been hired.

WARNING: **Keep sending out new applications to other companies until you have been on the job for at least a week.** Be especially wary of interviewers who say things like: "You seem great. I think you'd work out just fine. There's just one more person I want you to meet. She's in Seattle right now, so I'll give you a call and set something up after she returns." Be careful! You do not have an offer until you have negotiated terms and gotten something in writing, or you have been on the job for at least a week and everything is going well. Otherwise, you are still on the market and you had better keep creating job-search activity.

It is emotionally crushing to look for a job one promising opportunity at a time. This is a stupid, inefficient, and psychologically damaging methodology, yet many managers and executives do it. There are a thousand things that can go wrong with a placement decision, most of them completely outside your control. Here are some hiring stories from hell that have happened to clients of mine:

One hiring manager told my client to show up for work on a certain day. When she got there, the man who had hired her had been fired and no one knew her from Eve. They told her to leave.

One manager told a candidate that she was perfect for the job. The "hiring authority" asked for references, discussed salary and incept dates, and gave the impression that the deal was sealed. In a later meeting, this person admitted that she didn't have the authority to hire anyone, and the candidate would have to meet with a higher manager. That manager did not like the candidate at all.

One candidate got a letter of intent from a company, complete with salary, incept date, and relocation plans. Then, two days before he was to leave, the company called and said one of his references was bad. They chose to invoke a clause in the letter, "subject to satisfactory background check." He is suing

them, but meanwhile he is unemployed because he had given notice at the job he had. His career is seriously damaged.

Another candidate was hired to replace a key manager who was leaving the company after a long tenure. A week before she was to show up for training, she was informed that the manager had changed his mind about leaving, and was going to keep his position. She was "un-hired" in favor of the already-trained manager.

More than a few candidates have been involved in placement efforts that were aborted entirely. Sometime after a search was launched, the company changed its plans and decided not to hire anyone at all. Some of these candidates had been told that they were the company's "first choice."

Do not let up on your search activity until you have a firm offer. A firm offer is explicit, unequivocal, and comes complete with terms for salary, perks, and incept date. Until then, you want to have at least ten active leads going at all times, which means that you will need to be in contact with many dozens of companies simultaneously. Remember: No one application or rejection should define your search. *Do not look for work one lead at a time.* We'll come back to this in the next chapter.

Negotiating an Offer: Salary, Perks, Incept Date

If you think you are getting an offer, stop the interview and get serious: "Are you offering me the position?" If you get an unqualified "yes" in answer, then follow up with, "With what terms?"

If you think you are getting close to getting an offer, you can precipitate the event. Again, here are the closing lines from the last chapter: "Given what you know about me now, Ms. Johnson, is there any reason we couldn't work together?" Or, "Ms. Johnson, this job sounds perfect. What would I need to do to convince you to offer me this position?" It is even okay to be as direct as this: "Ms. Johnson, I've given you a pretty good idea of what I can do, and you've given me a very clear understanding of what you need. This looks like a match to me. Can we make a deal on this today, or is there something else you need from me to make your decision?"

(Remember, don't ask a yes-or-no question in negotiations, unless you can afford for the answer to be no.)

❋

As specified in the last chapter, you want to deflect salary inquiries until as late in the game as possible. If you can delay any serious salary discussions until after you have a job offer, then *you have already won the negotiation.* You have the offer. It's yours to decline. After they make an offer, you are no longer the seller, you are the buyer. The deal has been agreed to but the price has not yet been set!

Try to avoid getting entangled in negotiations over the phone. If they call you to make a job offer, and attempt to launch a discussion of salary and terms, say, "I think we can wrap this up better in person. Are you available tomorrow morning?" It's too easy for a hiring manager to give up on negotiations when you are *not* standing in her office. The last thing you want to hear is, "Mr. Cooper, it seems that you have higher expectations than we can meet. I thank you for your time. I guess we'll just have to let one of the other candidates take a shot at this."

Always negotiate cash salary first, then bring in other variables. For some new hires, the only variables will be salary and incept date. For others—such as executives at major corporations—there is a huge range of perks to be negotiated: signing bonus, performance incentives, golden parachute, pension guarantees, vacation, insurances, tuition for your children, child care, elder care, relocation expenses, trailing spouse services, stock options, investment planning, limousine or car service or company automobile, shower in your office, ad nauseam. You will never have more power over these matters than during the window of time between an offer and a handshake on the deal. For more on this, read Chapman's *How to Make $1000 a Minute,* or see chapter 13 of my book *The Overnight Résumé,* or chapter 18 of my book *From College to Career* (see Bibliography).

(One caution, contrary to what some career books say: Be careful about jacking up any salary offer to the absolute maximum possible. If you negotiate a salary one dollar less than the amount that would result in the offer being withdrawn, then you remove all room for error. You are selling your honeymoon period at the company for cash. If you don't deliver immediate results, you could find yourself in another job search—fast. If you are completely confident of your ability to deliver those results, this caution does not apply to you.)

Once you have negotiated salary and terms, get it all in writing. You don't need to ask for a contract or even for a formal letter. For the purposes of ensuring that you are talking about the same things, ask for a piece of company stationery, write down what you think you heard, and get the hiring manager to sign it.

Then, ask for a specific amount of time to consider the offer. If you anticipated this offer, fully considered every ramification, and predetermined a decision, it is fine to accept the offer in the meeting in which it is tendered. For most candidates, however, it is a good idea to think it over for at least a day or two. Do not make a vague request, as the company will be nervously awaiting your decision. Be this specific: "I would like to take three days to consider this, Walter. May I let you know my decision on Friday morning?" If a company is unclear on your intentions, or if you stall them too long, they may withdraw their offer *without even telling you.* No reasonable employer will refuse you a few days to consider an offer, but few will wait two or three weeks while you make up your mind. Remember, they have to stall all their other candidates while you are stalling them.

Once you have a firm offer, it is perfectly fair to call up all your other hot prospects and let them know that you have an offer. This may force them to tip their hands and make an offer also.

WARNING: You can only counter an offer with another offer! Never turn down an offer because of speculative interest on the part of another company. "We are really interested in you" doesn't mean a thing. "Let's get together at nine tomorrow and see if we can iron out a better offer than theirs" does. If you have to, you can call up the first employer and ask for a few more days to consider the matter.

Incidentally, do not accept a counteroffer from your own employer when you give notice. Even if they keep you, possibly with a hastily arranged raise, your loyalty will be compromised, and whatever forces caused you to be underappreciated or underpromoted will still exist. Out of the numerous times I have seen clients accept such a counteroffer from their own employer, I cannot think of one that has worked out to their benefit.

Once you accept an offer, you are off the market. As a matter of honor, you cannot accept another offer no matter how appealing it may be. Show the same integrity you would expect of an employer. The day after you formally accept an offer, call any other standing offers and politely decline, but don't completely shut down your job search yet! Reduce your activity to a lower level, but be sure to keep seeking out new contacts and compiling new leads. If you want to know why you should do this, reread the job-search disasters a few pages back. These people thought they had a done deal, too.

Only when you have been on your new job for a few days, and everything feels right, should you shut down your search totally. Send a note to every soul involved in your search and thank them warmly. Announce your appointment and provide your new business telephone number. Offer your services to help them in any way you can, should they ever need it.

Then, remember to keep your network alive. Don't wait until you need help again; make an occasional call. Your network can be your lifeline. As we have seen in this book, you don't need one to launch a job search, but it certainly makes it easier.

How to Snatch Victory from the Jaws of Defeat

If you are not selected for a specific job, do not despair. If you have become a finalist in a company's selection process, you have created a great networking contact. The hiring manager may even feel guilty about not being able to offer you the position, and that guilt can motivate her to help you.

If you are not hired, press for leads and referrals. Ask the hiring manager your "Who do you know. . ." questions. See if she can refer you to branch or division managers within her own company who may need someone like you. Remember, this hiring manager thought well enough of you to make you one of the finalists in her hiring project. This is an asset that you can use.

Most nonselected candidates slink off and sulk, but not you! Instead, write a short letter stating how delighted you are to have been considered by Megadiversicorp, a company you have always admired and respected. Let them know that should any need arise on their part for your services, you would be more than happy to meet with them again.

What if you decline an offer? Do the same thing. You didn't find a good match this time, but the right position might come up in the future, and you want them to know that you would be more than happy to be considered for it. Let them know why you are declining this particular offer, and let them know what kind of position *would* interest you. (If you decline an offer solely due to a meager salary offer, it's probably just as well to keep that to yourself.)

Then, check in with them on a regular basis. Be especially sure to call after their new hire has been on the job for three or four weeks. If the hire was a mistake, they will start to know it by then. If you sense that the placement might not stick, check in with them as often as possible, perhaps once a week.

What happens if you do this? Amazing things:

One candidate interviewed repeatedly for a purchasing manager's job. He was not selected, even though he was ridiculously qualified for the job, perhaps over-qualified. He let the employer know that he really liked the company, and was genuinely sorry they didn't have a match. He was pleasant, honest, and congenial. A couple of months later he got a call. They wanted him to interview for a job two levels up, division director of procurement, with higher pay, more responsibility, and better opportunity for advancement. He was hired.

This candidate had been unemployed for some time, and had decided to accept the purchasing manager's job if it had been offered. It's a good thing for both of them that it wasn't.

Another candidate was a finalist for an account rep position, but ended up being the hiring manager's second choice. The first choice hire worked out great, but the second choice candidate, Phil, kept calling every couple of weeks anyway. "How's everything going over there? You need any help yet?" One day the orders were piling in, somebody was out sick, and the hiring manager's phone rang. "Oh. Hi, Phil. What great timing. We're up to our elbows in alligators with no time to drain the swamp. Can you get down here tomorrow? Maybe we can work something out. Would you consider working on contract for awhile, until we see if this volume is going to continue?" Phil took that offer, and was later hired permanently.

This job was created for him because the employer had a need, and Phil was ready to step in and help out. Look at it from the hiring manager's point of view: Why launch another expensive and time-consuming search when someone like Phil—reliable, flexible Phil—is ready to come on board? Incidentally, do not be afraid to take contingent work. Estimates are that as many as one quarter of all civilian jobs are now contingent (part-time, contract, or temporary). Many of these jobs convert to full-time, permanent employment, and employers are far more likely to convert the incumbent along with the job than to launch a search for a new hire.

Another candidate made it all the way to the final heat for a position with corporate headquarters. He wasn't selected, but he wangled a referral to a branch manager in another city. When the branch manager heard he had been referred down from corporate headquarters, she hired him.

One candidate impressed a hiring manager, but she had no position available for
him. "Maybe you can help me another way. Who do you use as a headhunter?
This is a rather obscure line of work, and I haven't been able to find a headhunter
who specializes in it." She gave him the name of the headhunter she always used,
and permission to use her name. The headhunter, thinking the hiring manager
was calling in a favor, beat the drums until he came up with a placement for the
candidate.

Snatch victory from the jaws of defeat. Realize that those hiring managers who
don't hire you are perhaps the most important people in your network. Check back
in with hiring managers until they feel they know you.

A Success Story

Greg S. wanted to be a stockbroker with a top brokerage house on Wall Street. He
was referred by a mutual acquaintance to the firm's sales manager. Greg brought his
résumé down to the firm's headquarters to give to his acquaintance, Ted.

Instead of serving as his proxy, Ted walked him down to the sales manager's office
to introduce him in person. The sales manager, let's call him Spike, didn't even look
up. In a monotone he said, "Nice to meet you, Gregory. I don't have time to read your
résumé now. Why don't you try to call me on Monday." Notice that he said "try to
call me"; he didn't say he'd take the call.

Greg didn't wait until Monday; he called on Friday afternoon. "Spike, this is Greg
S. I have a really busy week next week. I'm not sure I can reach you on Monday. Did
you get a chance to read my résumé? Maybe we can talk now."

"Nope. Didn't get a chance to read it yet. Call me Monday."

Greg called him Monday, Tuesday, Wednesday, two or three times each day. Spike
never took the call.

Then Greg called Ted and got Spike's direct line. Greg started calling Spike at 6:00
A.M., 5:15 P.M., and lunchtime, but still, all he got was Spike's voicemail.

Finally, Greg caught him at 5:45 on Tuesday morning on his private line, before
his secretary came in.

"Hey, Spike. Did you get a chance to read my résumé?"

"Oh, yeah," said Spike. "You can have an interview tomorrow morning. Can you
be here at 6:00 sharp?"

Greg went in early the next morning. He was having a pretty good interview when
Spike looked up and said, serious as death, "You're not our type." Greg did not bat an
eye. "What exactly are you looking for?" he asked, and then went on to present evidence from his background that he was indeed their type. In the end, Spike was non-

committal. "Maybe you'd work out, but I don't know if I have a spot for you. I have to discuss this with my boss. I'll have to get back to you." Of course, he didn't.

Next week, it was more of the same. Spike didn't return Greg's calls or messages. Finally, on Wednesday, Greg caught him at the front door to the building at 5:45 A.M. "I was just having breakfast with Ted and thought I'd wait for you. What's the story, Spike? Have you had a chance to think it over? I know this could be beneficial for both of us. Here, I brought you my references. Why don't you call them? They'll tell you what you need to know." All Spike said to him was, "Why don't you come in tomorrow?" "What time?" Greg asked. "Anytime you like."

When Greg came in the next morning at 8:00, Spike said, "OK, you're hired."

Later on, Greg told this story to his new coworkers. "You know, I don't think Spike likes me," he said, and recounted the whole story of his hire. Several of the older brokers chuckled, while the younger ones all turned to each other and said, "That's funny, he did the same thing to me."

✺

The secret to Greg's success was persistence. "If he had told me that I didn't stand a chance, I would have dropped it, but he kept leaving me hanging," Greg told me later. "I couldn't just walk away from the lead without a clear answer."

Greg did everything right. He hand-delivered his résumé, turned a networking connection into a personal introduction, persisted past every screen to reach his decision-maker, overcame objections in the interview, and followed up to force the hiring manager to make a decision. You need to be prepared to do the same.

CHAPTER 8

Track and Troubleshoot Your Job Search

"In today's world security must flow from the individual not the job. Few jobs are secure; the only security derives from the ability to adapt and move."

—David Birch, *Job Creation in America*

Getting More Yesses

Some job-search strategies stress that you should expect to hear a string of "nos" in your job search. The point of this is to prepare you to expect rejection and to take it in stride. The theory is that with every "no" that you hear, you are one step closer to the "yes" you want.

While it is true that you will hear "No," "No," "No," "No" for the duration of your search, *do not fall in love with collecting "nos."* A much better pattern would be "No," "No," "No," "Yes," "No," "No," "No," "Yes," "Yes," "No," "No," "No," the right "YES." You need to get offers once in awhile to gain any practice at the endgame to the job search. If you are getting all "nos," you need to take another look at your job targets and your search tactics.

Don't buy into the theory that you need to kiss a lot of frogs to find a prince. You need to kiss a lot of princes to find the right one for you. Princes are job offers.

Would you marry the first person you ever kissed? I don't think so. Likewise you should be wary of accepting the first position you are offered, especially if that offer pops up very early in your search. You may sell yourself short or accept a poor match before you even test the market. On the other hand, if the offer looks good and satisfies your requirements, accept it and consider yourself lucky.

The old rule of thumb for computing the duration of a job search was to allow one month for every $10,000 in income. That's a rough rule to begin with, but search durations will vary wildly when you factor in regional and industry-specific economic trends, as well as each candidate's unique situation (credentials, education, mood, and demands for salary and working conditions).

One sign that your search is going well is that you will get offers fairly often. What does "fairly often" mean? That depends on your search. The higher up the ladder you go, the fewer offers you can expect. For the overwhelming majority of full-time jobseekers, however, if you aren't getting at least one solid, real, and viable offer per quarter, you need to evaluate your search itself.

Tracking Your Search

Operate your job search as if it were a job in and of itself. Set objectives each week, quantify and record your efforts and results, and use these data to analyze the cost-benefit of your tactics. Set performance standards as noted in the book; for example, return all calls within twenty-four hours, write thank-you letters and get them in the mail the same day as the interview, and so on. Above all, establish a regular job-hunting routine and stick to it.

If you are on vacation or unemployed, work at your job-search job for at least forty hours per week, from Sunday noon through Friday noon. If you are employed, you will need to work on your job-search job every evening and through the weekends. Also, if you are employed, you must find snippets of time throughout the business day to make phone calls—even if you have to sneak out and use the phone in the deli next door.

Set a goal of making a certain number of new applications every week. In my opinion, no one can run a job-search campaign who is not willing to initiate at least ten new applications per week. Even if you are employed at a demanding job, you can find time to contact at least ten new prospects every week. Remember, each new prospect generates continuing follow-through, so even ten new prospects a week will soon become a pretty large project as you call and develop names for decision-makers, mail out letters and résumés, follow up with telemarketing efforts, arrange meetings, research companies at the library, and put up with inevitable bouts of phone tag and other delays.

REMEMBER: A lead is only dead when you are sure it cannot produce a job offer for you *ever*. Then it becomes a networking lead. A networking lead is only dead when your contact tells you never to call him again as long as you live. A lead might stay active for months, as you wait for so-and-so to get back from vacation, for the quarterly budget to be approved, for the president to make up his mind, and so on.

Just ten *new* contacts a week could easily become over one hundred simultaneously active prospects. This is why you must diligently maintain your 5 × 8-inch lead cards, or the organizational challenge of your search will sink you. If you start missing deadlines and failing to return phone calls, you're going to miss offers you could easily have won.

The upper limit to new contacts must be set by you. Whatever upper goals you set, make sure you set a minimum for *new* contacts per week. Then, even during the weeks of Thanksgiving and your mother-in-law's annual visit, meet your goal for new contacts.

Other data you want to track is where those new contacts are coming from. Up to 50 percent of your leads can come from cold-calling and prospecting. Anybody with a telephone book and a quarter can prospect for a new job. Up to 50 percent can come from networking. As we have discussed in this book, even if you don't know a soul, you can create a network by prospecting. No more than 25 percent should come from headhunters and agencies. No matter what, no more than 25 percent should come from newspaper advertisements and other sources for announced openings.

Use the format on the following page to write up your Job Search Weekly Report. If you don't quantify your work, you can find yourself thinking you're "really busy" when no substantive job-search work has been accomplished. Prepare this report on Sunday evening, and if you are short of your minimum for new contacts, write some letters and get them in the mail.

Finally, track all your job-search expenses, including long-distance calls, transportation costs, and out-of-town meals. Many of these expenses are tax deductible (at least they were at the time this book went to press), but there are some quirks to the tax law. One of the quirks is that you have to be looking for work in the same field as the one you were last employed in. This book does not purport to give tax advice. A timely call to your accountant could save you significant tax liability, especially if your search is a long or expensive one.

Why Searches Fail

You need to track, analyze, and fine-tune your job search as it progresses. Even if your search is going well, it can always go better. Most searches fail because of one of three problems:

1. **Lack of effort**
2. **Faulty search process**
3. **Economic forces outside the control of the candidate**

If you are not working at your job search for forty hours a week, you need look no further than that for failure analysis. The worst search methodology in the world will

SUNDAY NIGHT SCORECARD - THE JOB SEARCH WEEKLY REPORT

LIST OF <u>NEW</u> CONTACTS: (ten minimum)
1)
2)
3)
4)
5)
6)
7)
8)
9)
10)
n)

NEW CONTACTS FROM NETWORKING:
(up to 50% of total effort)   _____   _____
                                                     number   % of total

NEW CONTACTS FROM COLD-CALLING:
(up to 50% of total effort)   _____   _____
                                                     number   % of total

NEW CONTACTS WITH HEADHUNTERS & AGENCIES:
(no more than 25% of total effort)   _____   _____
                                                     number   % of total

NEW CONTACTS FROM ADVERTISEMENTS:
(no more than 25% of total effort)   _____   _____
                                                     number   % of total

---

LIST OF FOLLOW-UP ACTIVITY: (should be more than one page, *at least*)

FIRST INTERVIEWS:

CALL-BACK INTERVIEWS:

OFFERS:

GOALS FOR NEXT WEEK:

eventually work if you will just pursue it for forty hours a week. Sending résumés and letters to ads in the newspaper *for forty hours a week* will land you a job relatively quickly. Hanging a large sign on your neck and handing out your résumé in the financial district *for forty hours a week* will get you a job long before you starve. Just think how effective the comprehensive, systematic search techniques espoused in this book will be if you employ them *for forty hours a week.*

If you work at your search diligently and consistently and you are not getting offers, then either your process is flawed, or economic forces outside your control are impacting your search. It is almost always the former. No matter how bad the job market is in your sector, people still quit, retire, get fired, transfer, get promoted, move to other cities following a spouse, or, if nothing else, die. Don't confuse job creation with the job market. Jobs change hands at a rate many times the rate of job creation. Even if the total number of jobs in a given sector is shrinking, jobs are still changing hands *every single day.* In a tight market, employment works like a game of musical chairs. The quick and the aggressive will win seats. The slow and the indecisive will not.

So, in the overwhelming majority of cases, job-search failure is due to lack of effort or a flawed search process. Effort has to come from you. This book is organized to present job-search processes in distinct phases. The six central chapters of this book correspond to the six phases of a job search. If you can identify the phase of your search that is flawed, you can use the appropriate chapter(s) to troubleshoot your search.

The Six Phases of a Job Search

1. **Identify One or More Precise Job Targets (chapter 2)**
2. **Identify Raw Leads (chapter 3)**
3. **Develop Raw Leads into Specific Names to Contact (chapter 4)**
4. **Turn a Name into an Appointment (chapter 5)**
5. **Sell in the Interview (chapter 6)**
6. **Close the Deal (chapter 7)**

As your search progresses, reread specific chapters as needed to refine and troubleshoot your search. If one single job in your sector changes hands, you deserve to win it.

❊

Many searches fail because the candidate has chosen a target for which she is not appropriately prepared. Reread chapter 2, "Identify One or More Precise Job Targets." If the market in your field is really tight, you may have to be satisfied with a lateral move. Targeting a job more than one step down from the one you have will create a host of difficulties, starting with that interview stopper, "It seems you're overqualified." Trick résumés can go a long way toward solving that problem; read my book, *The Overnight Résumé.* Whenever you are researching an industry, try to identify the growth niche. For example, recently, even as architectural firms were laying off architects right and left, they were trying to recruit designers with a specialty in medical spaces; as corporations were releasing recruiters from human resources' staff, they were recruiting organizational development specialists to help them with restructurings.

Some candidates "run out of things to do" because they cannot identify enough leads. Reread chapter 3, "Identify Raw Leads," and then check out the appendix, "Resources You Can Use to Research Potential Employers." If there are very few employers in your area who might hire someone like you, you must either develop every single one of them, look in a wider geographic area, or broaden your job target. No candidate should ever "run out of things to do" in a job search!

Many job searches fail because the candidate flits from lead to lead without any cumulative learning process taking place. Pursue leads systematically. Call up employers and ask them what they are looking for. Call back employers who don't hire you and ask them to comment on your résumé and your candidacy. Use language like this: "I understand that you probably had very good reasons for the choice you made, and I don't resent it at all. That's your job, to make those kinds of tough decisions. May I ask your help, though, in improving my jobseeking skills. Can you tell me why you didn't hire me? And please be honest." Ask them how you can overcome any shortcomings. Then use that intelligence in your next contact with that same kind of employer. If you are interested in a particular type of job, discover every single employer in your area who might be able to hire you, and apply to them sequentially until you have applied to every single one, then check back with them every ten days until somebody needs your help. Flitting from lead to lead, especially if you flit from announced opening to announced opening, keeps you from improving a thing about your candidacy. Never pass up an opportunity to turn one lead into several just like it. One history professor obtained an appointment to interview with an elite private college. There were several other colleges nearby, so he called them up and arranged interviews with them as well. Not one of them was hiring, or so they said, but they were willing to meet with him anyway. The college that flew him out did not extend an offer, *but one of the ones that wasn't hiring did.* As this story illustrates, no line of work is too conventional for these techniques.

If you suspect that employers think you are too old, buy stylish clothes that fit, and alter your résumé by dropping the dates off your education and only giving ten or fifteen years of experience. Be energetic, talk about what you can do, describe the benefits of your experience, and allay the employer's fear that you will be too expensive or inflexible. Pay attention to style. Have the latest style of résumé, know the latest buzzwords, have a haircut from this decade, read the latest information in the trade press, be up-to-the-minute on your field. Books on this topic include Morgan's *Getting a Job After Fifty*, Ray's *Job Hunting After 50: Strategies for Success*, Birsner's *The Forty Plus Job Hunting Guide*, and, to a lesser extent, Ramos' *The Joy of Job Hunting.*

If you are not getting in front of enough interviewers, your search will take much longer than it has to. You absolutely must meet in person with hiring authorities to get a job offer. Reread chapter 4, "Develop Raw Leads into Specific Names to Contact," and chapter 5, "Turn a Name into an Appointment." Get out of your passive mode and show some initiative! Start calling and asking for interviews, or you may wait forever for your next position.

If you are always a bridesmaid and never a bride, that is, if you find yourself repeatedly one of the finalists but never the one who gets the job offer, then you are blowing either your interviews or the job-search endgame. Reread chapter 6, "Sell in the Interview," and chapter 7, "Close the Deal." You need to research companies more carefully before you go into the interview, you need to state your interest unequivocally, you need to follow up precisely, you need to perform some task to prove your competence, and you need to show enthusiasm for the opportunity. (I had a client once who complained that a résumé I had written for him was not working. "How many interviews have you gotten?" I asked. "About fifteen," he said. "And how many résumés have you mailed out?" I asked. "About seventy." "You ought to bronze that résumé," I told him. "That's a great résumé. I don't know what you are doing in those interviews, but that résumé is a winner.")

If you feel employers' attitudes about your lack of education are hurting you, you are wrong. It is *your attitude* about your lack of education that is hurting you. Realize that employers hire people they like whom they think can do the job. Reread chapter 5, "Turn a Name into an Appointment," and go out there and get some interviews. If an employer likes you and thinks you can do the job, that's a match. Whenever you see notices in announced ads "college degree required" or "advanced degree preferred," *just ignore them.* Apply anyway, get on the phone and get an appointment, and show the employer who you are. Better yet, get out of the ads altogether, develop your own interviews, and get to an employer before she can write one of those ads.

If you have no related experience, use a similar technique. Take your background, job by job, and break it down into functions. Then, highlight the functions that are required in your targeted job. Rewrite your résumé to emphasize the functions that matter in your targeted industry. This can distort the appearance of your background, but if everything you say is true, go with it. Remember to consider what skills your volunteer background, education, early jobs, and home life might illustrate. Also, pick up some related classes, even if they are just one-day seminars and workshops offered through the local university extension or adult education program. Then take responsibility for developing your own interviews. You'll get a job.

If you are looking out of state, schedule interview junkets. Identify and develop potential employers, then tell them you will be in town only briefly. Represent yourself as an elite property, and let them know that you are definitely relocating. You are not "considering relocation," you are definitely relocating. Get them to interview you whether they are hiring or not, using the techniques in chapter 5, "Turn a Name into an Appointment." Take a vacation or otherwise arrange a trip. If you are financially able, consider moving there without a job. This takes guts, but it is actually the most successful method.

If you have been self-employed, use résumé tricks to disguise that fact (again, see *The Overnight Résumé*). Once you are in the interview, do not hide the fact you were self-employed, but overcome the employer's fears that you will be hard to manage by emphasizing your collaborative management style, committee work with professional associations, and volunteer work with and for others.

If you have a lot of education and little or no experience, read *From College to Career*.

If you work in a dying industry, then you have some serious decisions to make. First of all, accept that it is your responsibility to manage your career. Because of the accelerating changes in the economy, workers who have spent many years building careers can suddenly find themselves expert in a job that doesn't exist any more. History is littered with industries that died, replaced by something that was faster, easier, better, cheaper, or, increasingly, exported to countries where labor, *even brain labor*, is faster, easier, better, cheaper.

If your industry is on the wane, you can choose to fight for one of the fewer and fewer jobs available. Using the methods in this book, you can win the very last musical chair. If your industry is suffering from a *temporary* decline, even a severe one, you most certainly should sit it out. Find a safe harbor and wait for the next upturn. If, however, your industry is on a permanent decline, you probably should get out of it. If you are smart and motivated, why should you spend years of your career in an industry with no potential?

Your choices: Look for work nationally and be willing to move anywhere you can find a job. Lower your standards for salary or level of responsibility. Get some advanced or specialized schooling, either to augment your desirability in the current market or to redirect your career into a new market. Consider a related industry using the same skills and knowledge base. Segue into an unrelated industry, using the function you currently perform as a stepping stone (see p. 10). Use volunteerism to develop skills in a new function or industry. Start your own business. Retire. All of the above.

Don't wait around for a government or industry grant for retraining. You'll probably die first.

✳

Every jobseeker should constantly analyze and improve her interviewing skills, collaterals (letters and résumés), and techniques for accessing decision-makers and for turning mutual interest into job offers. Whenever possible, associate with other jobseekers. Meet once a week to share tips and tactics, and for emotional support. Read job-search books; you don't need to read every word, just skim them for the sections most pertinent to you. Here's a suggestion you won't hear everywhere: Read sales books. Go into the nearest good business bookstore and buy two or three books on sales techniques or motivation. These books are much better than most job books at providing tips you can go out and use the next day. If you are management level, be sure to read the *National Business Employment Weekly* (call 800-JOB-HUNT). The job-search articles are invaluable, whether you use the ads or not.

A comprehensive, systematic job search is a big operation. You may want to cut corners and listen to advice that seems easier, but if you want to get the best job you can in the shortest time, then don't fool around. As the saying goes, "Nothing succeeds like excess."

The Psychology of a Job Search

Everyone who has ever been unemployed for an extended period of time thinks his is a uniquely awful experience. In fact, not only did several people have the experience before you, but millions of people are having the experience with you. Right now.

If you lose your job, there are certain, predictable psychological stages you will experience. Knowing what to expect can help lessen the deleterious aspects of unemployment.

First of all, you may feel disoriented and confused. Americans, unlike most of the rest of the world, tend to equate their identify and their worth with their jobs. Do you think your value really changed when you lost your job? It did not. You can counter this effect somewhat by working on your résumé, making lists of career contributions and other accomplishments in your life.

Some candidates, especially those who did not see the separation coming, spend time entertaining feelings of self-pity and worthlessness, blaming *themselves* for the separation, alternated with intense and obsessive anger at the former employer, blaming *them* for the separation. All candidates may feel that they have let their families down, they may feel guilty at not working and not earning, and they may experience self-anger. It is common to feel irritable, frustrated, and moody, even around those who are trying to help you most. It is extremely important that you not stay in this stage for too long. If you need to, seek professional help. Seeing a career counselor, a career psychologist, or a regular psychotherapist for awhile will be more than worth the expense. Try to avoid getting involved in deeper explorations, say, of feelings about your father, and if you don't like one therapist or counselor, stop seeing that one and find another. You want to focus on career issues, get out of your funk, and get your job search back on track. You can worry about your father later.

Alternately, many candidates go through an initial period of excessive optimism. They think they will find a job in "no time." This optimism usually lasts until their first rejection for a job they really think they should have won. Then they run the risk of sliding into the despair mentioned above.

At some stage many candidates withdraw from their friends and families, isolating themselves, perhaps hiding their joblessness from others, and generally doing the opposite of what it takes to run an effective job-search campaign. This stage is particularly difficult on your spouse, who more than anything wants to help. The physical manifestations of this stage are that you may tire easily, you may engage in alcohol or drug abuse, or enter the perils of daytime TV (which is practically the same thing). While you are in this stage, you may be particularly resistant to job-search advice from others, and you may ignore good tips and leads, telling yourself that they are chimerical and there is no use pursuing them anyway. You will run a disjointed campaign during this stage, seeing no relationship between one job-search activity and another, and building no momentum even when things do accidentally go well. Feelings of hopelessness and/or helplessness are normal and common, but should never be allowed to dominate one's psyche.

Then, you come out it. Believe it or not, you do not stay in a state of despair forever.

You come out of it and joblessness, and your job search, become normal. You settle into a rhythm. You start to ask for and accept help from your friends, family, and acquaintances. You renew your commitment to find a position commensurate with your abilities, and you are effective at planning and conducting your search. You may continue to be angry and frustrated, but you will probably be able to control these emotions and use them as fuel for your search, rather than letting them sap your energy.

How long does each stage last? That depends on you. Your goal, obviously, is to weather these predictable stages as smoothly as possible, to listen to your contacts and *not pass up a promising lead,* and get to the final stage, viewing your job search as your normal life, as quickly and painlessly as possible.

After that, you run a new risk, that of losing your creativity and doggedly pursuing search techniques that don't work. Be careful that you don't fall into a pattern of failure, doing what doesn't work only because it is the most familiar to you. Keep trying new things, reading new books, exploring new career directions, taking new risks. Make yourself keep working the telephone, instead of retreating into a direct-mail campaign with one-tenth the efficacy of a comprehensive search methodology.

Always be willing to try something new, create more options, try something you haven't considered before. If you've only been applying to Fortune 500 companies, apply to start-ups. If you only applied to line jobs, apply for related staff jobs. Try a related industry, or consider companies in a broader geographic area, or apply for government jobs. Whatever you do, don't keep doing the same old thing over and over again if it's not working.

A job search requires almost infinite amounts of self-motivation. If you get stuck, break your search into minute tasks. Create control by concentrating on small steps, and give yourself rewards for every little step completed. (As soon as I write three letters I'll make that sandwich. I'll read the sports page as soon as I have marked ten ads that look promising. I'll go for a run after I make three more phone calls.)

Above all, hope is imperative to a job-search campaign. To maximize hope, try to maximize the number of viable applications you have going at any possible moment. Remember the three tenets driving and guiding your search:

○ **No technique works 100 percent of the time.**

○ **No one application or rejection should define your job search.**

○ **Your goal is to improve your odds on *every* application.**

Run your job search like a business. Pursue your outside activities and avocations, but don't let them interfere with your search anymore than you would let them interfere with a career job. Don't take a lot of little vacations that interrupt the rhythm of your search. Be sure to exercise, spend time with your friends and family, and stay away from drugs, alcohol, and mindless television.

You can beat the psychological challenges of an extended job search by reaching out to others for help, accepting that help when it is offered, realizing that your worth is intrinsic, and keeping hope alive every day by keeping a good volume of applications going *at all times*.

I once knew a poet who kept ten poems in the mail at all times. He was rather well known, actually, but he still got far more rejection slips than publishing dates. He told me that he didn't mind getting a rejection letter at all, because he still had nine poems out there that were going to win the Pulitzer Prize.

Good luck, and may you win the Pulitzer Prize for job searching.

*Until one is committed
there is hesitancy, the chance to draw back,
always ineffectiveness.
Concerning all acts of initiative (and creation)
there is one elementary truth
the ignorance of which kills countless ideas
and splendid plans:
That the moment one definitely commits oneself
then Providence moves too.
All sorts of things occur to help one
that would never otherwise have occurred.
A whole stream of events issues from the decision
raising in one's favor all manner
of unforeseen incidents and meetings
and material assistance
which no one could have dreamt
would have come one's way
Whatever you do or dream you can, begin it.
Boldness has genius, power and magic in it.
Begin it now.*

—Goethe

Resources You Can Use to Research Potential Employers

Information to Buy

As mentioned earlier, you can buy information on companies. Dun & Bradstreet Information Services, just as one example, can provide you with names of officers, multiple telephone numbers, information on sales and sales trends, and addresses *for nine million companies.* At the time this book went to press, they had a $300 minimum, but if you sorted the data on multiple criteria and added in officers and phone numbers, the minimum order jumped to $1000. Nevertheless, management and executive jobseekers who want instant access to thousands of potential employers might consider buying data to jump-start their job search. However, Dun & Bradstreet data do not cover startups and companies too small to need a credit rating. In some industries and in some areas of the United States, that will be the majority of potential employers. Dun & Bradstreet Information Services' phone numbers are 201-605-6000 or 800-624-5669. Two companies providing similar data are Seagate Associates, 201-262-5200 or 800-992-5520, and Finders/The Advantage, 301-788-0500 or 800-628-9685. You can search on-line database services yourself. As mentioned earlier, the nearest major library may have database services, for free or for a fee. Call them, or check in *The Fiscal Directory of Fee-Based Information Services in Libraries* (published by FYI, a department of the County of Los Angeles Public Library, 310-868-4003 or 800-582-1093).

The rest of the materials in this chapter provide data the old-fashioned way—in books. Some of these books you can buy, but many are prohibitively expensive and can best be found in the reference section of the nearest library. Some are out of print, but worth the trouble of locating at a used bookstore or, again, at the local library.

Books on Books

These books can help you find obscure newsletters, directories, industry guides, trade press, and career books.

Job Hunter's Sourcebook: Where to Find Employment Leads and Other Job Search Resources. Michelle LeCompte, ed. Detroit: Gale Research Inc., 1991.

Encyclopedia of Business Information. 9th ed.

Where to Start Career Planning: Essential Resource Guide for Career Planning and Job Hunting, 1991-1993. 8th ed. C. Lindquist and D. Miller. Princeton, N.J.: Peterson's Guides, 1991.

Directories in Print. Detroit: Gale Research, annual.

Guide to American Directories. B. Klein, ed. West Nyack, NY: Todd Publications, biannual.

Business Periodicals Index. Bronx, NY: Wilson Publishing, annual.

Encyclopedia of Business Information Sources. Detroit: Gale Research, biannual.

Books on Jobs

If you want to explore career options, these books are a good place to start. If you already know what kind of job you want, skip to the next section.

Dictionary of Occupational Titles. 3 vols. New York: Gordon Press, 1991.

The Enhanced Guide for Occupational Exploration. M. Maze and D. Mayall. Indianapolis: JIST Works, 1991.

Straight Talk on Careers: 80 Pros Take You into Their Professions. M. Barbera-Hogan. Garrett Park, MD: Garrett Park Press, 1987.

The Encyclopedia of Career Choices for the Nineties. New York: Walker and Co., 1991.

Offbeat Careers: The Directory of Unusual Work. A. Sacharov. Berkeley, CA: Ten Speed Press, 1988.

The Book of U.S. Government Jobs: The U.S. Government Employment Guide. 4th rev. ed. D. V. Damp. Corapolis, PA: D-Amp Publications, 1991, 412-262-5578.

The Almanac of American Government Jobs and Careers. R. L. Krannich and C. R. Krannich. Manassas, VA: Impact Publications, 1991.

International Jobs. E. Kocher. Reading, MA: Addison-Wesley Publishing Co., Inc., 1990.

The American Almanac of Jobs and Salaries. J. Wright and E. J. Dwyer. New York: Avon Books, 1990.

Where the Jobs Are: A Comprehensive Directory of 1200 Journals Listing Career Opportunities. Norman Feigold and Glenda A. Hanjard-Winkler. Garrett Park, MD: Garrett Park Press, 1989, 301-946-2553.

Books on Companies

Before visiting any company, you should know how big it is, when it was founded, what its products and key technologies are, what its recent sales trends have been, and who its major competitors are. You can start with books like these, and then go on to check newspapers and business periodicals for recent articles or citations. You can also use books like these to compile your initial target lists. Be sure to note the next section, which will allow you to research the *people* in these companies. There are many, many more resources than this available at a good business library. These titles are only provided as a place to *start* your research.

> Your Local Telephone Company's Yellow Pages Directory. Note: some airports and libraries have telephone directories from major cities nationwide.
>
> *America's Fastest Growing Employers.* Holbrook, MA: Bob Adams, Inc., 1992.
>
> *Everybody's Business: A Field Guide to the 400 Leading Companies in America.* M. Moskowitz, et al. New York: Doubleday, 1990.
>
> *The 100 Best Companies to Work for in America.* R. Levering, et al. New York: New American Library, 1987.
>
> *The Best Companies for Women.* B. Zeitz and L. Dusky. New York: Simon & Schuster, 1988.
>
> *Standard & Poor's Register of Corporations, Directors, & Executives.* New York: Standard & Poor.
>
> *America's Corporate Families & International Affiliates.* (formerly *Billion Dollar Directory*). Mountain Lakes, NJ: Dun & Bradstreet, annual.
>
> *Directory of Corporate Affiliations.* 2 vols. Wilmette, IL: National Register Publishing Company, annual.
>
> *Corporate 1000 and International Corporate 1000.* Washington, D.C.: Monitor Publishing, date not set.
>
> *Ward's Business Directory.* Belmont, CA: Information Access.
>
> *Million Dollar Directory Series.* Parsippany, NJ: Dun & Bradstreet.
>
> *Standard Directory of Advertisers: Geographical Edition.* Wilmette, IL: National Register Publishing Company.
>
> *Standard Directory of Advertisers: Tradename Index.* Wilmette, IL: National Register Publishing Company.

Additionally, there are many guides to companies in specific locales or industries. In order to find out if there is such a guide for your particular industry or targeted locale, you will need to check with a good librarian or book dealer (one who will take the time to actually search a subject for you instead of just a title or author).

> *Career Opportunities in Television, Cable, and Video.* 3rd ed. M. K. Reed and R. K. Reed. New York: Facts on File Publications, 1990.

How to Get a Job with a Cruise Line. Rev. ed. M. F. Miller. St. Petersburg, FL: Ticket to Adventure, 1992.

Jobs in Paradise: The Definitive Guide to Exotic Jobs Anywhere. J. Maltzman. New York: Harper & Row, 1990.

Career Opportunities in the Sports Industry. S. Field. New York: Facts on File Publications, 1991.

Commerce Register's Geographical Directories of Manufacturers (for various locales and metropolitan regions nationwide). Midland Park, NJ: Commerce Register, various publication dates.

Thomas' Register of American Manufacturers. New York: Thomas Publishing.

State Manufacturing Directories. Vary by state, but every state has one.

Aerospace Companies. Greenwich, CT: DMS, Inc.

American Apparel Manufacturers Association Directory. Arlington, VA: AAMA.

American Electronics Association Directory. Palo Alto, CA: AEA.

The Biotechnology Directory. New York: Stockton Press.

Broadcasting and Cable Market Place. Washington DC: Broadcasting Publications, Inc., annual.

Chain Store Guides (numerous). New York: Business Guides Inc., (212) 371-9400.

Chemical Industry Directory. New York: State Mutual Book and Periodical Service, Ltd.

Data Sources—The Comprehensive Guide to the Information Processing Industry. New York: Ziff-Davis].

Directory of Hotel and Motel Systems. New York: American Hotel Association Directory Corp.

Insurance Almanac. Englewood, NJ: Underwriter Printing and Publishing.

International Directory of Marketing Research Houses (aka *The Green Book*). New York: American Marketing Association.

Telephone Industry Directory & Source Book. Potomac, MD: Phillips Publishing.

Working Press of the Nation. Burlington, IA: National Research Bureau, 1990.

World Directory of Pharmaceutical Manufacturers. London: IMS World Publications.

Books on People

Whenever you are researching a company to approach them about a job or in preparation for an interview, look up the company's top officers in a "Who's Who"-type directory. Knowing where your targeted interviewer or the president of the company went to school or got her early industry experience can be a surprising advantage.

Standard & Poor's Register of Corporations, Directors, & Executives. New York: Standard & Poor.

Who's Who in America. Wilmette, IL: Marquis.

Who's Who in Finance & Industry. Wilmette, IL: Marquis.

Who's Who in Venture Capital. D. A. Silver. New York: John Wiley & Sons, 1986. O.O.P.

National Directory of Addresses and Telephone Numbers. Kirkland, WA: General Information.

National Roster of Realtors Directory. Cedar Rapids, IA: Stamats Communications, Inc.

Rand McNally Bankers Directory. 3 vols. Chicago: Rand McNally.

Reference Book of Corporate Managements: America's Corporate Leaders. 4 vols. Parsippany, NJ: Dun & Bradstreet.

BIBLIOGRAPHY

Suggested Further Reading

Résumés

The Overnight Résumé. D. Asher. Berkeley, CA: Ten Speed Press, 1991.

From College to Career: Entry-Level Résumés for Any Major. D. Asher. Berkeley, CA: Ten Speed Press, 1992.

The Damn Good Resume Guide. Rev. ed. Y. Parker. Berkeley, CA: Ten Speed Press, 1989.

Designing Creative Resumes. Rev. ed. G. Berryman. Los Altos, CA: Crisp Publications, Inc., 1991.

Cover Letters

200 Letters for Job-Hunters: Every Possible Way to Get Job Offers. W. Frank. Berkeley, CA: Ten Speed Press, 1990.

Dynamic Cover Letters: How to Sell Yourself to an Employer by Writing a Letter that Will Get your Résumé Read, Get You an Interview . . . and Get You a Job! K. Hansen with R. Hansen. Berkeley, CA: Ten Speed Press, 1990.

The Perfect Cover Letter. R. Beatty. New York: John Wiley & Sons, 1989.

Job-Search Guides

The 1993 What Color Is Your Parachute? R. N. Bolles. Berkeley, CA: Ten Speed Press, 1993. (Revised annually.)

Who's Hiring Who? R. Lathrop. Berkeley, CA: Ten Speed Press, 1989.

Telesearch: Direct Dial the Best Job of Your Life. J. Truitt. New York: Collier Books (Macmillan), 1983. O.O.P.

Guerilla Tactics in the New Job Market. 2nd ed. T. Jackson. New York: Bantam Books, 1991.

Not Just Another Job. T. Jackson. New York: Random House, 1992.

The Very Quick Job Search. J. M. Farr. Indianapolis, IN: JIST Works, 1991.

Get the Right Job in 60 Days or Less. R. H. Beatty. New York: John Wiley & Sons, 1991.

The Job Search Handbook: The Basics of a Professional Job Search. J. Noble. Holbrook, MA: Bob Adams, Inc., 1988.

Job Hunting After 50: Strategies for Success. S. N. Ray. New York: John Wiley & Sons, 1991.

Getting a Job after 50. J. S. Morgan. Blue Ridge Summit, PA: Tab Books Inc., 1990.

The Forty-Plus Job Hunting Guide: Official Handbook of the Forty-Plus Club. Rev. ed. P. Birsner. New York: Facts on File Publications, 1990.

The Joy of Job Hunting. B. Ramos. Sherman Oaks, CA: Somar Press, 1989.

Go Hire Yourself An Employer. R. Irish. Garden City, NY: Anchor Books (Doubleday), rev. ed., 1978.

Hot Tips, Sneaky Tricks & Last-Ditch Tactics: An Insider's Guide to Getting Your First Corporate Job. J. Speck. New York: John Wiley & Sons, 1989.

The Berkeley Guide to Employment for New College Graduates. J. Briggs. Berkeley, CA: Ten Speed Press, 1984.

300 New Ways to Get a Better Job. E. Baldwin. Holbrook, MA: Bob Adams, Inc., 1991.

Jobs for English Majors and Other Smart People. 3d ed. J.L. Munschauer. Princeton, NJ: Peterson's Guides, 1991.

Life After Shakespeare: Careers for Liberal Arts Majors. M. Flores-Esteves. New York: Penguin Books, 1985.

Harvard Guide to Careers. New ed. M. P. Leape and S. M. Vacca. Cambridge, MA: Harvard University Press, 1991.

Marketing Yourself: How to Use State-of-the-Art Sales and Marketing Techniques to Enhance Your Value in a Rapidly Changing Business World. D. Leeds. New York: HarperCollins Publishers, 1991.

The Job Search Organizer. J. O'Brien. Washington, D.C.: Miranda Associates, Inc., 1990.

The Complete Job-Search Handbook. Rev. ed. H. Figler. New York: Henry Holt and Co., 1988.

The Only Job Hunting Guide You'll Ever Need. K. Petras and R. Petras. New York: Poseidon Press, 1988.

The Perfect Follow-Up Method to Get the Job. J. G. Allen. New York: John Wiley & Sons, 1992.

The Ex-Inmate's Complete Guide to Successful Employment. E. C. Sull. Buffalo, NY: Aardvark Publishing, 1990.

Headhunters

The Headhunter Strategy: How to Make It Work for You. K. Cole. New York: John Wiley & Sons, 1985.

Rites of Passage at $100,000+: The Insider's Guide to Absolutely Everything about Executive Job-Changing. J. Lucht. New York: The Viceroy Press, 1988.

The Director of Executive Recruiters. Fitzwilliam, NH: Kennedy Publications, annual, 603-585-2200 or 603-585-6544.

The Recruiting & Search Report (a constantly updated database). Panama City Beach, Fl.: K. Cole and Company, 904-235-3733 or 800-634-4548 to order custom sort printouts.

Hunting the Headhunters: A Woman's Guide. D. Cole. New York: Fireside (Simon & Schuster, Inc.), 1988.

How to Get a Headhunter to Call. H. Freedman. New York: John Wiley & Sons, 1989.

The Career Makers: America's Top 100 Executive Recruiters. J. Sibbald. New York: Harper & Row, 1990.

Interviewing

Sweaty Palms: The Neglected Art of Being Interviewed (revised). H. A. Medley. Berkeley, CA: Ten Speed Press, 1985.

Information Interviewing: What It Is and How to Use It in Your Career. M. Stoodley. Garrett Park, MD: Garrett Park Press, 1990.

Knock 'em Dead: With Great Answers to Tough Interview Questions. M. J. Yate. Boston: Bob Adams, Inc., 1990.

How to Make $1000 a Minute: Negotiating Your Salaries & Raises. J. Chapman. Berkeley: Ten Speed Press, 1987.

The Five-Minute Interview. R. H. Beatty. New York: John Wiley & Sons, 1986.

The Ultimate Interview. J. Caple. New York: Doubleday, 1991.

More Career Books of Interest

Where Do I Go from Here with My Life?: A Very Systematic, Practical, and Effective Life/Work Planning Manual for Students of all Ages, Instructors, Counselors, Career Seekers and Career Changers. J. C. Crystal and R. N. Bolles. Berkeley, CA: Ten Speed Press, 1974.

The Three Boxes of Life and How to Get Out of Them: An Introduction to Life/Work Planning (rev. ed). R. N. Bolles. Berkeley, CA: Ten Speed Press, 1981.

Discover What You're Best At: The National Career Aptitude System and Career Directory. B. Gale and L. Gale. New York: Simon & Schuster, Inc., 1982.

Do What You Love—The Money Will Follow: Discovering Your Right Livelihood. M. Sinetar. New York: Dell Publishing, 1987.

Work with Passion: How to Do What You Love for a Living. N. Anderson. New York: Carroll & Graf Publishers, Inc., 1986.

Blow Your Own Horn: How to Market Yourself & Your Career. J. Davidson. New York: Berkley Books, 1987.

The Experienced Hand: A Student Manual for Making the Most of an Internship. 2d ed. T. Stanton and K. Ali. Cranston, RI: Carroll Press, 1987.

Great Careers: The Fourth of July Guide to Careers, Internships, & Volunteer Opportunities in the Nonprofit Sector. D.C. Smith. Garrett Park, MD: Garrett Park Press, 1990.

The Peace Corps and More: 114 Ways to Work, Study, and Travel in the Third World. M. Benjamin. Cabin John, MD: Seven Locks Press, 1991.

Career Burnout: Causes & Cures. A. Pines and E. Aronson. New York: Free Press (Macmillan), 1988.

Unnecessary Choices: The Hidden Life of the Executive Woman. E. Gilson with S. Kane. New York: Paragon House, 1989.

The Best Companies for Women. B. Zeitz and L. Dusky. New York: Simon & Schuster, 1988.

The Executive Odyssey: Secrets for a Career Without Limits. F. G. Harmon. New York: John Wiley & Sons, 1989.

The Joy of Working. D. Waitley and R. Witt. New York: Ballantine Books, 1985.

Before You Say "I Quit!" D. Holloway and N. Bishop. New York: Collier Books, 1990.

Stay or Leave. B. Gale and L. Gale. New York: Harper & Row, 1989.

The Perfect Job Reference. J. G. Allen. New York: John Wiley & Sons, 1990.

Secrets of the Hidden Job Market. B. Rogers, S. Johnson, B. Alexander. White Hall, VA: Betterway Publications, Inc., 1986.

Beyond the Uniform: A Career Transition Guide for Veterans & Federal Employees. W. D. Lee. New York: John Wiley & Sons, 1991.

Developing Your Career as a Scientist in Academe. G. Moser. Cambridge, MA: Harvard University Office of Career Services, 1989. Available by phone order only: 617-495-2595.

Preparing for Your Academic Career in the Humanities and Social Sciences. C. Packert and M. Leape. Cambridge, MA: Harvard University Office of Career Services, 1989. Available by phone order only: 617-495-2595.

Choosing an Academic Career. M. Leape and W. Hunt. Cambridge, MA: Harvard University Office of Career Services, 1988. Available by phone order only: 617-495-2595.

Working. S. Terkel. New York: Ballantine Books, 1972, 1974.

Job Creation in America: How Our Smallest Companies Put the Most People to Work. D. Birch. New York: Macmillan Inc., 1987.

Sales & Motivational Books

Cold Calling Techniques: (That Really Work!). 3d ed. S. Schiffman. Holbrook, MA: Bob Adams, Inc., 1990.

Streetsmart Teleselling: The 33 Secrets. J. Slutsky and M. Slutsky. Englewood Cliffs, NJ: Prentice-Hall, 1990.

Power Talking: Fifty Ways to Say What You Mean to Get What You Want. G. Walther. New York: Putnam Pub. Group, 1991.

Phone Power. G. Walther. New York: Berkeley Pub. Group, 1987.

Ziglar on Selling: The Ultimate Handbook for the Complete Sales Professional. Z. Ziglar. Nashville, TN: Oliver-Nelson, 1991.

The First Five Minutes: The Successful Opening Moves in Business, Sales & Interviews. N. King. New York: Prentice-Hall, 1989.

Sell Like a Pro: The Buyer Friendly Approach to Sales. S. Estes. New York: Berkeley Pub. Group, 1990.

Zapp! The Lightning of Empowerment. W. C. Byham with J. Cox. New York: Harmony Books, 1988.

Conceptual Selling. R. Miller and S. Heiman with T. Tuleja. New York: Warner Books, 1987.

Ten Greatest Salespersons: What They Say about Selling. R. L. Shook. New York: Harper & Row, 1978.

How I Raised Myself from Failure to Success in Selling. F. Bettger. New York: Simon & Schuster, 1982.

Guerrilla Marketing. J. C. Levinson. Boston: Houghton Mifflin Co., 1985.

Guerrilla Marketing Attack: New Strategies, Tactics & Weapons for Winning Big Profits. J. C. Levinson. Boston: Houghton Mifflin Company, 1989.

The 7 Habits of Highly Effective People. S. R. Covey. New York: Simon & Schuster, 1989, 1990.